"*Reaching Single Adults* is an important book that needs to be read by every pastor and Christian educator, as well as by every parent of a single adult who is concerned by the marginalization of the unmarried in the body of Christ. Dennis Franck does not just rehearse the problem or lambast church leaders. He passionately offers solid, seasoned guidance on how to reach America's greatest mission field. Only a leader long in this field could have written such a resource for effective ministry."

Harold Ivan Smith, speaker and author

"Dennis Franck uses his years of experience to lay a firm foundation for a local church to begin ministry to the single adults in its community. Readers will gain a wealth of information based on Franck's research as well as his practical experience. With the increasing single adults population and the seemingly decreasing attention given by churches to single adults, *Reaching Single Adults* is a must read for church leaders."

Linda G. Hardin, general coordinator, single adult ministries, Church of the Nazarene

"Dennis Franck has been at the forefront of singles ministry since the beginning. When you read *Reaching Single Adults* you will understand why. It is practical in its application but personal in its perspective and will become the new standard for this vital area of ministry."

Earl Creps, director of doctoral studies, Assemblies of God Theological Seminary

"My reward in life is watching individuals and churches effectively provide practical ministry. At last, a comprehensive guide for ministry to single adults. Dennis Franck not only ignites passion for single adult ministry but also opens the toolbox to accomplish the task. With over 40 percent of our communities being single, this is a must read for anyone desiring to reach single adults."

George E. Krebs Jr., Christian education director, Pennsylvania-Delaware District Council

"Ministering to the unique needs of single adults was one of the first written challenges of the early church. Today, the rapid growth of the single adults population has brought greater problems and challenges. Dennis Franck, an apostle and prophet called and sent to minister to single adults, has chronicled some practical tools to help churches and ministries reach and minister to their single adults. This book is a must read for all churches interested in reaching the largest population group in America."

Daniel J. Vassell Sr., crosscultural youth/singles ministries coordinator, Church of God International Youth and Christian Education Department

REACHING SINGLE ADULTS

An Essential Guide for Ministry

DENNIS FRANCK

BakerBooks

Grand Rapids, Michigan

© 2007 by Dennis Franck

Published by Baker Books
a division of Baker Publishing Group
P.O. Box 6287, Grand Rapids, MI 49516-6287
www.bakerbooks.com

Printed in the United States of America

Library of Congress Cataloging-in-Publication Data
Franck, Dennis, 1951–
    Reaching single adults : an essential guide for ministry / Dennis Franck.
        p. cm.
    Includes bibliographical references.
    ISBN 10: 0-8010-9190-X (pbk.)
    ISBN 978-0-8010-9190-2 (pbk.)
    1. Church work with single people. I. Title.
BV639.S5F73 2007
259.086′52—dc22   2006026117

Contents

Acknowledgments

I would like to acknowledge the people who have been influential in my life and ministry with single adults. Without these individuals, I would not have had the degree of personal growth and development I've experienced through the tremendous opportunities and fulfilling times in ministry to single and single-again people since 1978.

To my wife, Jill—thank you for always listening to my gripes, groans, and questions (sometimes late at night!), for being my sounding board, confidant, advisor, and personal cheerleader during the challenging times of ministry to and with the thousands of single adults with whom God has enabled us to meet, teach, counsel, guide, and develop fulfilling relationships. I know God has given me a wise, caring, loyal wife in you. Thanks for being who you are to me, and to others!

To the hundreds of volunteer leaders who have worked alongside me in our ministries in Milwaukee; Billings, Montana; Omaha; San Jose; Boise; and Dublin, California—thank you for the dedication to your specific ministries, passion for reaching and discipling single adults, and loyalty to me as a leader, even when I did not exhibit all the qualities a leader should possess. You helped make our ministries effective, need-fulfilling, and relevant to single adults who came through our doors.

To the thousands of paid and volunteer leaders, authors, counselors, and consultants working with single adults in churches and parachurch ministries—thank you for what you do! You are helping to reach and shape the lives of single and single-again adults for the glory of God and the benefit of people. You are in the trenches of ministry! By ministering to and with people who have never been married, are divorced or divorcing, are widowed, are single-parent or blended families with biological, step, or adopted children, you are dealing with almost every challenging issue the church faces today. By your ministry to, for, and with single adults, you portray strength, willingness to risk and learn, courage, and an attitude of fun and growth. I commend you! In my opinion, you are heroes in the faith.

Introduction

As a former full-time singles pastor to the never-married, divorced, widowed, separated, and single parents in six Assemblies of God churches since 1978, I was keenly interested in the opportunity to research and write on the topic of single adult ministry. I also saw it as an excellent way to provide a training course for existing and potential leaders in single adult ministries. Another motivation for writing this material was the additional learning that would benefit my ministry as the director of single adult/young adult ministries for the Assemblies of God.

Past, Present, and Future Need for Training

Since beginning ministry to single adults in 1978, I found no targeted training for single adult ministry in the Assemblies of God until 2000, and there was little training in other church groups until the late 1980s. Certain groups such as Single Adult Ministries (now Strategic Adult Ministries affiliated with David C. Cook Ministries), NSL (Network of Single Adult Leaders), and various other denominational groups (e.g., Southern Baptist, Presbyterian, Reformed Church of America) offered some training in those early years (1975–1985); however, it was limited.

I remember traveling to the Crystal Cathedral in Garden Grove, California, in 1981 to attend a three-day national leadership training seminar for Single Adult Ministries. There I mixed with hundreds of leaders from various parts of the country representing many church backgrounds. I became acutely aware of the massive need for targeted ministry to single and single-again adults of all ages and was educated concerning the *who, what, when, where, why,* and *how* of ministering to them.

Another national training conference I attended was sponsored by Ward Presbyterian Church in Livonia, Michigan, in 1983. This Presbyterian church knew how to attract and retain single adults and taught the nuts and bolts of ministry to them. These two events provided the first organized training I received to assist me in this diverse ministry to the five types of single adults: the never-married, divorced, widowed, single-parent, and separated persons.

Since beginning the Single Adult/Young Adult Ministries Office in 2000 for the national headquarters of the Assemblies of God, I have found, in my efforts to discover a course of this type in any of our twenty-one Assemblies of God colleges, that not one of them has such a class. The closest courses in any of our colleges resembling even a hint of specific training in understanding and ministering to single and single-again persons are classes entitled "Church Ministries" (or something similar). These classes examine children's, youth, men's, women's, family, missions, music, Christian education, sometimes single adult, and the many other ministries in the church today in an overview form. A quick look at each of these, usually one sixty-minute class per ministry group, is provided to educate and acquaint the student with the many ministry opportunities and challenges in the church today.

This format is at least a start, but it is hardly adequate in preparing a pastor, associate pastor, or Christian leader in understanding and effectively ministering to the diverse needs of single and single-again persons of all ages. Since 2002 the Assemblies of God national Single Adult/Young Adult Ministries Office has offered regional conferences for single adults and young adults with leadership training in both ministries to attempt to meet the dire need. Various books, videos, and digital leadership resources have also been gathered, produced, promoted, and sold by the national office and leaders across the country to address this need for education and training.

Training the Credentialed Minister and Lay Minister

Admirable as these efforts are, they are not nearly enough! One author stated the need and opportunity for training well when he said, "Out of the divorces, widowhood, the singles bars, clubs, apartments and condominiums, comes a torrent of need, and it is flowing right past the door of our churches. . . . There is boundless talent and creativity in this flood of single adults. The church can help and it can also be helped. It can give and it can receive. *Opportunity is there. What will we do?*"[1]

I wholeheartedly agree with these comments! It is time, even past time, for the church in the United States to become aware of and involved with the numbers, needs, and issues of the single and single-again people all around us. We need to develop a mentality of acceptance, wholeness, and *ministry to, for, and through* this ever-increasing segment of society. It is time for the church to think new thoughts and to be bold and creative as it reaches out to an increasingly *nonfamily community*.

Another book for training pastors, associate pastors, and lay leaders in understanding the challenges of single adults will not saturate the market. Even if their churches do not have targeted ministry groups for single adults or young adults of any age, senior pastors desperately need to understand the diverse and complex issues of the never-married, the formerly married, the separated, the widowed, and single-parent individuals, as well as the families they represent. The age span of those people who would potentially attend and be involved in a specific ministry group covers at least fifty years, ages eighteen to sixty-eight. And as will be seen, the complex needs represented by single adults and their families include almost every issue in the church today! Certainly every senior pastor will, at some point, minister to one or more types of single adults.

Introduction

There is also a stark need to provide opportunities for training people who will be on a church staff as *single adult ministers, whether paid or volunteer.* Many Bible colleges train individuals for youth ministry, children's ministry, music ministry, missions ministry, and pastoral ministry. Why not train for single adult ministry? Why not raise the awareness of the need for specific training to reach this burgeoning population, now 96 million?[2] Why not offer targeted training to individuals to recognize, reach, restore, and release single adults to become more like Jesus, the greatest single adult who ever lived? Certainly single adults warrant our training, time, prayer, and efforts in ministry!

The Possibilities and Potential of Single Adult Ministry

Let's define the term *single adult.* I am referring to unmarried adults, ages eighteen or older, who happen to be single by *chance, change, circumstance,* or *choice,* whether theirs or someone else's choice. They fall into one or more of the following broad categories depending on their life experiences:

1. Never married
2. Formerly married (divorced)
3. Widowed
4. Single parent
5. Separated (the separated person is legally married but living a single lifestyle)

As a singles pastor for twenty-one years, I have had individuals from each of these backgrounds, as well as people who are single because of experience in two, three, four, or all five of the backgrounds. Single-again people who were part of our ministries were married one, two, three, four, five, even six times! Men and women widowed three or four times have become involved in many of the groups I have had the privilege of pastoring. Separated individuals, confused, hurting, and not knowing if or when they may get back together with their spouse, have come, some reluctantly, others willingly. Over the years young adults in their twenties and adults in their thirties, forties, fifties, sixties, and even seventies who had never married have made their way into our many groups targeted to single adults.

The point is this: single adults represent a variety of ages, have a multiplicity of life experiences, and face a diversity of challenges. These individuals are sometimes *lost in the crowd* in our churches due to a host of reasons, which we will come to see and understand. The opportunity to reach and teach them is all around us for the taking. Some churches from many denominations, as well as independent churches, are doing a good job of recognizing, reaching, restoring, and releasing single adults into the kingdom of God. I have been involved with many of these groups and can attest to this.

Why should churches not reach this huge segment of society, now 44 percent of all adults in the country ages eighteen and older?[3] Why should we not position ourselves to reach a lost and dying world through them? Why should not our churches benefit from the tremendous abilities, talents, time, and other resources these unmarried individuals possess? Why should not our churches be enriched, impassioned, empowered, and blessed by the masses of the never-married, formerly married, widowed, separated, and single-parent individuals who walk in our church doors but, to the dismay of many leaders, walk out because we fail to understand, target, and disciple them?

It is possible to change the unfortunate tide of ignorance and misunderstanding! It is possible to dismantle the myths and negative stereotypes that exist in many of our churches. It is possible to attract and retain hundreds of thousands of single and single-again adults for the kingdom of God. Pastors, church leaders, and parachurch ministry leaders need to realize that:

- Our Christian faith is based upon a *Jewish single adult* from Galilee,
- Whose ministry was preceded by a single adult named *John the Baptist*,
- Whose mission thrust was modeled by a single adult named *Paul*.

The individual who reads and utilizes this book will be able to articulate a biblical and practical philosophy for single adult ministry, gain an overall understanding of the diverse needs of single and single-again adults, understand various models of ministry, and learn how to organize, begin, and run a diverse, effective single adult ministry. This person will also learn how to identify, recruit, train, and motivate effective leaders, understand the reasons for and types of a wide range of programs, events, and activities that are necessary in a ministry to single adults, and have at his or her disposal a list of resources. The objectives of this book are to provide the principles and knowledge to:

1. Understand singleness in the Old and New Testaments.
2. Outline a philosophy for ministry to and with single adults.
3. State and describe important principles that will help a church minister to and with single adults.
4. Understand the diverse needs of single adults.
5. Explain why a single adult ministry is needed in the local church.
6. Identify and describe seven ministry models.
7. Outline and discuss a variety of programs.
8. Examine and summarize the primary characteristics of single adult ministry.
9. Relate the basic steps in beginning a single adult ministry.
10. Outline how to identify, recruit, train, and motivate leaders and leadership teams.
11. List and evaluate available resources relevant to single adult ministry.

PART
ONE

Foundation of Single Adult Ministry

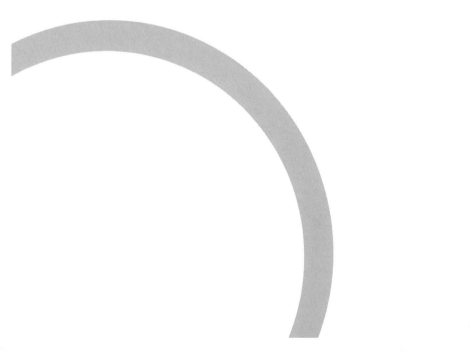

Every building needs a foundation. Without it, the structure would collapse under its weight due to not having enough support underneath. The foundation determines the size of the building, the strength of the building, and whether it will last. The same is true of this book, which is designed to acquaint individuals with ministry to single and single-again adults and to train leaders for ministry to and with them. Without a proper comprehension of the target audience (the never-married, divorced, widowed, single-parent, and separated individuals), the reasons for this ministry, and an understanding of how the church can minister to single adults, this book would be of little value. It is with these principles in mind that this was written.

Objectives of This Section

The following objectives frame the structure of part 1 of this book.

1. *Gain a biblical understanding of singleness in the Old and New Testaments.* There are many people in the Bible who lived successful single lives. There are many individuals whom God used in ways he may not have been able to had they been married. There are many leaders whom we may not have realized were single or single-again due to death of a spouse or death of a marriage.
2. *Understand a philosophy of ministry to and with single adults.* The philosophy for ministry to single adults gives specific principles and values of why it is so desperately needed in the church today. It also provides insight into the reality of what happens when the needs of single adults are not addressed by the church.
3. *Explore principles that will help a church minister to single adults.* Any church can minister to single adults, even if it is only in becoming aware of and sensitive to their needs and issues. This is just the beginning, however. Most churches can go far beyond this and provide compassionate, biblical, targeted ministry to the single adults of at least one of the three age groups and three need groups presented and discussed.

The vast majority of evangelical and Pentecostal churches of any denomination are "marriage and family focused." That in itself is not a bad posture. Most Christian leaders understand the importance of marriage and the church's role in strengthening the family unit. *The unfortunate reality, however, is that our marriage and family emphasis many times does not include single adults.* This is not necessarily by design but is often by ignorance and neglect.

In the United States singleness due to chance, change, or choice has continued to grow over the years and is now approaching one of every two adults. Due to the death of one's spouse, the practice of marrying later, divorcing sooner, and other cultural practices, I believe it is a phenomenon that is here to stay. We should not be so surprised when we realize that:

- In the beginning, the first humans were created single (Gen. 2:7, 21–22).
- In the end, we will all be either single or single-again in heaven (Matthew 22:30).
- In between, God sent a single adult to save us (John 1:12).

Biblical Perspectives on Singleness

Objectives

1. Identify and describe the major prophets of the Old Testament who were single and the reasons for their singleness.
2. Examine the eunuchs, priests, rabbis, and Essenes in the Old Testament and their relation to singleness.
3. Summarize the three types of eunuchs Jesus referred to in the New Testament.
4. Identify five probable characteristics of the person who has the gift of singleness.
5. Demonstrate that Jesus was a single adult while on the earth.
6. Demonstrate that Paul was a single adult and summarize three probable reasons he preferred singleness.
7. Discuss and distinguish between the teaching of Jesus and of Paul concerning the gift of singleness.

My research has discovered that the study of singleness in the Bible is mostly an unexplored topic. *The Interpreter's Dictionary of the Bible*, for example, has only a small article on celibacy, one expression among others of the single life. The *New Catholic Encyclopedia* devotes a total of nine pages to two articles on the subject, "Canon Law of Celibacy" and "History of Celibacy."[1]

Due to tragic events concerning sexual molestation that have taken place in the Roman Catholic priesthood and due to the major role celibacy has played in this faith for many years, celibacy is now being fiercely debated. It is probable that some who devote themselves to the priesthood and a life of sexual abstinence do not, in fact, have the "gift of singleness," which, I believe, helps one to live a chaste life. (This gift will be addressed later.) Protestants are also reexamining the option of singleness due to the ever-growing numbers of single and single-again adults in the United States (44 percent of all adults age eighteen and older).[2]

The Old Testament

The fact that marriage was divinely ordained and normative in early Israel was well accepted and understood. Genesis 1:26–28 and 2:4–25 show God's intentions for man and woman to marry, multiply, and fill the earth. The mating of male and female and the creation of offspring was seen as normal and expected for all created life (Gen. 1:22, 24). Singleness was not given a place of honor, acceptance, or authority in the Old Testament.

It was considered shameful for a woman to be unmarried and without a child. In Genesis 30:22–23 we read that when God opened Rachel's womb so she could bear a child, she said, "God has taken away my reproach" (RSV). The story of Jephthah also illustrates this shame by showing the anguish of his daughter as she spent two months bewailing the fact that she would die without ever marrying (Judg. 11:37–40). Other Scriptures such as Isaiah 4:1 and 54:4 support this truth. "Life was seen as endowed and commissioned by the Creator to reproduce itself."[3]

Single Prophets in the Old Testament

Though it appears to have been a prescription of God to marry and reproduce, and although the subject of singleness is not discussed in the Old Testament, there are several examples of significant, prominent unmarried people (single for various reasons) whom God used in the Old Testament to fulfill his purposes. Three of these were the prophets Jeremiah, Ezekiel, and Hosea.

Jeremiah was commanded not to marry. "Then the word of the LORD came to me: 'You must not marry and have sons or daughters in this place'" (Jer. 16:1). God's command to Jeremiah to stay single was not really a rejection of marriage but, rather, was a judgment upon a historical situation or perhaps was a priority because of a particular circumstance. It is not known if the restriction to not marry was ever removed; however, it is clear that Jeremiah was one example of a great prophet who was single.

Marital status did not seem to be of great importance in the life of *Ezekiel* either, whose wife was taken suddenly from him by the Lord. He was not even allowed to weep or mourn but had to continue in the ministry God had assigned him (Ezek. 24:15–18).

The prophet *Hosea* experienced a broken marriage (divorce) but still continued a recognized ministry. God told him to marry a whore, Gomer, whom God knew would later leave Hosea for other men, illustrating the one-sided love that God had for Israel (Hosea 1–3).

In all three of these examples, Jeremiah's, Ezekiel's, and Hosea's marital status was not an issue for effective ministry. God was interested in the prophet's integrity, obedience, and ability to say what God wanted him to say. God's apparent prescription for man to be married now seemed to have exceptions.

Eunuchs in the Old Testament

Another example of singleness in the Old Testament is the eunuch. A eunuch in Byzantine and Mesopotamian times was a person who was castrated as a means of punishment. The Assyrians' practice of this cruel treatment dated back to the second millennium BC.[4] Eunuchs were commonly employed as servants or supervisory officials in the women's quarters of royal households, but they also served as bodyguards, palace officials, statesmen, and military officials.[5] Greek historian Xenophon reported that it was the belief of a Persian king, Cyrus the Great, that emasculation yielded more docile and easily managed slaves who, undistracted by family ties, were characterized by single-hearted loyalty in the palace and unquestioned fidelity in the harem.[6]

The use of eunuchs appears in several places in the Old Testament. The Hebrew term for eunuch, *saris*, appears forty-seven times.[7] Twenty-eight of those are translated by the RSV as "eunuch," but the others are called "military officer," "political official," or "chamberlain." The New English Bible translates the word as "eunuch" consistently. Scriptures referring to eunuchs include, among others: Isaiah 56:3–5, in which the reference is to an emasculated male; 2 Chronicles 18:8, in which the *saris* functions as an emissary for Ahab; 2 Kings 8:6, in which another is appointed by the king to restore lost property to the woman of Shunem; and Genesis 40:2, in which Pharaoh's chief butler and baker are eunuchs.

The Priests in the Old Testament

Nowhere in the Old Testament is there a clear command that priests should marry; however, the hereditary and perpetual nature of the Aaronic priesthood seems to imply that priests did marry. Furthermore, there are no allusions to unmarried priests in the Old Testament. It can certainly be inferred that priests should marry by the instructions governing marriage, but this is not explicit.

When Moses was instructed to speak to the priests, the sons of Aaron, he prescribed various regulations, including some details pertaining to marriage. "The woman he [the priest] marries must be a virgin. He must not marry a widow, a divorced woman, or a woman defiled by prostitution, but only a virgin from his own people" (Lev. 21:13–14). This seems to clearly prescribe qualifications for a priest's wife, but it does not require marriage in all cases. The Israelites could have considered it a command to marry, or they may have simply assumed the fact of marriage. Whatever the case, these governing guidelines are clear examples of descriptive language pertaining to a specific situation, time, audience, and culture for individuals aspiring to priesthood.

How different this practice is from today's norm for Catholic priests, who are expected to remain single for the work of the Lord and his church. This elevation of celibacy became more pronounced during the second century, due in part to a reaction against the licentiousness of the Greco-Roman world and, in part, to the influence of Gnostic dualism. By the fourth century some councils of the Western church were forbidding marriage after ordination as well as forbidding conjugal intercourse to those who entered the priesthood married. It seemed to be a natural progression to prescribe celibacy for the clergy, which became the rule in the West.

The Eastern church, however, maintained that priests and deacons may marry before ordination but not after. Absolute celibacy was required only of the bishops. This difference is an example of discontinuity between the Old and New Testaments, especially in the years immediately following the writing of the New Testament.

The Essenes in the Old Testament

The Essenes were a Jewish religious community that flourished in the first centuries BC and AD. According to Philo of Alexandria, the Essenes devoted much time to the study of moral and religious questions, renounced both women and money, and practiced celibacy: "Of the Essenes, none takes a wife."[8] In another instance Philo writes that the Essenes eschew marriage because they clearly discern it to be the principle danger to the maintenance of communal life, as well as the fact that they particularly practice continence.[9]

Some think the foundation of the Essenes was near the Dead Sea and, therefore, was not conducive to marriage and family life. Pliny locates the Essenes just west of the Dead Sea (probably the Qumranites) and also describes them as *sine ulla femina*, "without any women." He agrees with Philo and Josephus that the Essenes renounced sexual desire, and he only recognizes one group of the Essenes.

Josephus is probably closer to the truth because he recognizes more than one order of Essenes, each with different practices in marriage. In one statement he writes, "Marriage they disdain, but they adopt other men's children, while yet pliable and docile, and regard them as their kin and mould them in accordance with their own principles. They do not, indeed, on principle, condemn wedlock and the propagation thereby of the race, but they wish to protect themselves against women's wantonness, being persuaded that none of the sex keeps her plighted troth to one man."[10]

I find his opinion rather humorous, but the issue of whether marriage was the norm or the exception among the Essenes will not be settled easily. For those in this group who did marry, however, their celibacy was apparently vocational. They were volunteers for the Lord and subject to the disciplinary demands of holy war legislation of the Torah, which made it advisable for long-term enlistees to avoid marriage (Deut. 23:9–14). This correlates with Leviticus 15:16–18, which indicates that a man was unclean after copulation with his wife until he washed himself and it became evening.

Rabbis in the Old Testament

Rabbis in the Old Testament did not encourage celibacy but, in fact, desired marriage for a man by the time he was eighteen. They saw marriage as normal and proper for all people. They believed that an unmarried man should not be a teacher of children, nor should a woman be a teacher of children. Jesus, however, was called "Rabbi" by his followers and others in the New Testament (John 1:38, 49; 3:2; 6:25), and there is no biblical evidence that he was married. I believe he was single until his death at age thirty-three. It should be noted that in spite of all the evidence that marriage seemed to be the norm for rabbis, nowhere is there a specific command that a rabbi had to be married.

The New Testament

Despite the fact that marriage was still seemingly normative and served as a model of the relationship between Christ and his church in the New Testament, there is a substantial amount of material in the New Testament that addresses singleness. There are also a great number of individuals whom the text either says were unmarried or who definitely seem to be single due to a lack of any reference to a spouse. One is also led to believe these individuals apparently stayed single the rest of their lives. Singleness in the New Testament is given an honorable place of highest authority in both example and teaching.

Eunuchs in the New Testament

Jesus taught about three types of eunuchs in Matthew 19:12. The disciples were discussing marriage and divorce with Jesus. He explained that whoever puts away his wife and marries another, except for the cause of fornication, commits adultery. His disciples reacted, saying if this is the case it would be better not to marry. Christ ignored their possibly cynical attitude and ignorance and stated that abstaining from marriage is only for "those to whom it has been given" (Matt. 19:11). Simply stated, Christ was referring to those who are given the call and the grace to abstain from marriage.

The *International Critical Commentary* makes an excellent point regarding this: "It is clear . . . the disciples, instead of receiving an explanation and solution of their difficulty that marriage without facility for divorce would be a burden, receive what amounts to a commendation of abstention from marriage for the kingdom's sake. In other words, while verses 1–9 are calculated to heighten the conception of marriage, verses 10–12 are clearly intended to *increase respect for those who renounce marriage.*"[11]

Jesus notes three classes of men to whom it is given not to marry:

1. Those eunuchs who were so born and were probably physically unable to consummate marriage or who had the ability but lacked the inclination[12]
2. Those who were made eunuchs by men and were physically castrated
3. Those who made themselves eunuchs for the kingdom of heaven's sake

Succinctly stated, the ability to have a physical union can be summarized in this way. The men who were so born *cannot because of birth circumstances*. The men made eunuchs by others *cannot because of physical circumstances*. The men who made themselves eunuchs for the kingdom of heaven's sake *will not because of volitional circumstances*.

The Gift of Singleness in the New Testament

It is interesting that Jesus added the third type of eunuch to the list. This kind of eunuch was not mentioned or illustrated in the Old Testament, unless Jeremiah the prophet is considered to have been a eunuch for the kingdom's sake and had the gift of singleness. Although God actually told him not to marry, it is possible and even probable that God equipped him with this gift. The same could be said regarding Ezekiel after his wife died.

The point is that in the New Testament, Jesus taught on the issue of singleness, something not seen in the Old Testament, and actually called it a gift as marriage is a gift. Matthew 19:11 says, "Not everyone can accept this word, but only those to whom it has been given." Then in verse 12, "The one who can accept this should accept it." Because of a different culture, time, audience, and location, Jesus was addressing and expanding an issue that had become contemporary and relevant. He felt it imperative to do so. In the Old Testament the singleness of the prophets is descriptive in nature. In the New Testament, Jesus's teaching was prescriptive for the current time and culture. I believe his teaching regarding the person who has chosen to make himself or herself a eunuch for the kingdom of heaven's sake is also prescriptive for today (although the word *eunuch* is rarely used).

I strongly believe the *gift of singleness* Jesus refers to is a valid, credible, and biblical gift that is alive and resident in the lives of *some* single adults today. Although probably a very small percentage of single adults actually have this gift, *it is necessary and wise to teach it from a biblical perspective along with the gift of marriage*. It is possible that some who have remained single for many years may, in fact, have the gift of singleness and don't know or understand the gift. They could benefit greatly from biblical teaching on this subject.

The United States is increasingly becoming a nation of single adults due to the realities of individuals marrying later and divorcing sooner. The average first marriage in the United States lasts eight years, while the average second marriage lasts six years.[13] American culture postpones marriage until an average age of 27.1 for men and 25.4 for women, a five- and four-year increase respectively since 1970.[14] These demographics alone stress the fact that single adults desperately need and deserve this relevant biblical information and instruction concerning singleness.

Paul and the Gift of Singleness

The gift of singleness is also addressed by Paul: "I wish that all men were as I am [single and self-controlled]. But each has his own gift from God, one has this gift, another has that. Now to the unmarried and the widows I say: It is good for them to stay unmarried as I am. But if they cannot control themselves, they should marry, for it is better to marry than to burn with passion" (1 Cor. 7:7–9).

What is Paul saying? The apostle wishes that all had the ability to remain single like he is for the following reasons:

1. *To avoid the troubles* in life that stem from marriage (7:28)
2. *To be free from the concerns and anxieties* that arise from the demands placed upon spouses to care for each other (7:32–34)
3. *To devote oneself totally to the Lord,* using wisely the extra time that results from not having to care for a spouse (7:35)
4. *To be happier,* because Paul thinks the widow(er) would be happier in remaining unmarried (7:39–40)

Let me offer some concluding observations that have surfaced during my twenty-one years of ministry as a singles pastor to literally thousands of single and single-again adults. The following characteristics seem to be true of the person who possesses the gift of singleness:

1. He or she has reached a place of contentment in being single.
2. He or she does not struggle with the need for sexual satisfaction.
3. He or she is not overly concerned with having a romantic relationship.
4. He or she gives little thought to marriage.
5. He or she finds much satisfaction in using spare time to serve the Lord.

Jesus, the Single Adult

It is most likely true that Jesus remained single during his thirty-three years on the earth. There have been attempts, however, to deny this. William E. Phipps suggested that Jesus was married in his article written in 1968 entitled, "Did Jesus or Paul Marry?"[15] This article was followed by a book entitled *Was Jesus Married?* in which Phipps analyzed the question thoroughly in the context of the sexual attitudes prevalent in ancient Judaism and the silence of the New Testament on the issue. He concluded the New Testament assumes that Jesus had a normal sex drive and lived with the sexual identity of a male, both of which were needed elements for humanness and requirements to marriage.

Phipps went on to list ways that these biosocial qualities were indicated (in his opinion) and concluded that Jesus was married and participated in sexual relations! He then added a statement that could have been his motivation for study. "If such an opinion becomes widely endorsed it should have a beneficial effect on the Christian church and on the quality of life that western man idealizes as truly human."[16]

I cannot resist the urge to say this statement reeks of arrogance, bias, and a judgmental attitude, and it is totally misleading and undeniably false! I have ministered to and with many single and single-again adults who, like Jeremiah, Ezekiel, Hosea, Jesus, the apostle Paul, John the Baptist, Mary, Martha, Lazarus, not to mention Mary Magdalene, Timothy, Titus, and others, were examples of godly, influential, effective people who changed the course of history as single adults. Their marital status had nothing to do with God's accomplishment of significant ministry through them. Their *singleness actually enhanced the opportunity* for God to do great things in and through their lives (1 Cor. 7:32–35).

There is not a need to prove Jesus was married because of an opinion that marriage is the proof of an ideal or fulfilling life. Being "complete in him" alone is proof of a fulfilling life (Col. 2:10 KJV). Thus, believing the ludicrous opinion Phipps purports would not have a beneficial effect on the Christian church.

"Phipps used the silence of the New Testament as a platform from which to leap from his assumptions to his conclusions."[17] Yes, it is probable that Jesus had a normal sexual desire (he was human as well as divine). It is also possible that Jesus could have participated in marriage if he had so desired. The fact that these possibilities existed, however, does not necessitate a conclusion that Jesus was actually married. Would a wife of Jesus have been left out of the Scripture? I don't think so!

The book *The Da Vinci Code* and the recent movie by the same name attempt to prove the theory, among others, that Jesus was married to Mary Magdalene. The author and producers endeavor to produce proof that Christ filled the role of a husband and lived the life of a married man. Though some would choose to accept the theory, I do not.

The silence of the New Testament lends more support to the claim that Jesus was single than it does to the possibility that he was married. His full, busy, effective ministry life was probably one of the best reasons for remaining single. It is appropriately mentioned here again that Paul states in 1 Corinthians 7:32–35 that for ministry's sake, it is better to be single than married. Jesus, by not marrying, did not prescribe singleness for all of us. His example, however, certainly validates singleness as a viable and credible option.

Paul, a Single Adult

There really is no concrete biblical evidence showing Paul's marital state during his entire adult life. It is clear, however, that he was not married when he wrote 1 Corinthians 7:1–40, since he states that he wishes the unmarried and the widows could remain unmarried as he is (v. 7–8). In verses 25–26 he concludes that it is better for a virgin to remain single because of the present crisis. This pertains to both male and female as clarified in verse 29: "From now on those who have wives should live as if they had none."

Paul probably preferred singleness for himself for several reasons:

1. *Paul realized marriage is not for everyone and that singleness is a viable option.*[18] The myth that a person is somehow incomplete until married still exists in a majority of U.S. evangelical churches today. Many times there is a negative, suspicious, hurtful stigma concerning the person who has not yet married by the age of thirty (sometimes even younger). This suspicion seems to become stronger the longer a person stays single. Again, we would do well to remember the words of Paul in Colossians 2:10, which announce, "You are complete in him" (KJV).

2. *Paul chose to be single because it freed him to better accomplish God's will for his life.*[19] The incredibly tumultuous and time-consuming life of ministry Paul led would probably have been too much for a wife to bear. He would also not have had as much time to spend on ministry had he been married.

3. *Paul could develop more meaningful relationships than if he were married.*[20] Paul realized the need for close relationships could be met outside of marriage. Paul was constantly referring to "my co-workers," "my brothers," and so forth. The last chapter of Romans mentions twenty-seven names of friends, most with a special word about them.

In view of Paul's strong preference of the single life for himself and others, it is *extremely intriguing* that many church leaders have made him the chief authority for the "husband of one wife" test for a minister receiving credentials and appointments of elders and deacons (1 Tim. 3:2, 12; Titus 1:6). It is also noteworthy that interpreting this phrase the way many do eliminates all females and all single people. In fact, this would have excluded Paul himself, Jeremiah, John the Baptist, Jesus, and others!

I believe the fact that Paul was single and recommended it for others is applicable today. Paul's comments concerning singleness show unity with the comments of Jesus in the New Testament. He goes a step further than Jesus, though, by expounding on the subject to include widows and the unmarried as well as other remarks regarding divorce and marriage.

Other New Testament Single Adults

John the Baptist had the lifestyle of an ascetic but did not impose it upon others. He lived a simple life, yet he was used by God to forecast the coming of the Messiah. There is no mention of him ever marrying.

It is generally thought *Mary and Martha* were also single. There is no hint of a husband for either of them, and only their brother, Lazarus, lived with them. Ironically, there is no trace of him having a wife. Possibly their marital status is not an issue in the New Testament, but whatever the case, their lives show that people have identity apart from marriage.

Anna was an example of a female, single adult preacher. Luke tells us that she was a prophetess and a widow of about fourscore and four years who did not depart from the temple, serving God with fasting and prayers day and night. The fact that she was a preacher is seen in the words, "She . . . spake of him to all them that looked for redemption in Jerusalem" (Luke 2:36–38 KJV).

Frank Stagg points to the fact that Philip the evangelist "had *four virgin daughters* who were prophesying"[21] (Acts 21:9, emphasis mine). The word for preaching used here is *propheteuousai*, one of several used in the New Testament. Interestingly, being single or female does not appear to be an issue for ministry of this magnitude. The mention of "virgin daughters" could be seen either as an exception to the norm or an emphasis on singleness.

Lydia is possibly another example of a prominent single adult in the New Testament (her marital status is not mentioned). She was the mainstay for the church in Philippi at its founding (Acts 16:11–15) and was a blessing to Paul and his companions by providing hospitality to them.

There are many other adults in both the Old and New Testaments who were definitely single and others who were probably single. Those in the New Testament include:

The *Samaritan woman* who had five husbands was now single again (John 4:1–26).

Timothy, the author of 1 and 2 Timothy, was probably single.

Titus, the author of the book of Titus, was probably single.

Mary Magdalene, who reported Jesus's empty tomb, was probably single (Luke 24:10).

Those in the Old Testament include:

Deborah, Rebecca's nurse who never had a family of her own but found fulfillment in her work, apparently stayed single (Gen. 24:59; 35:8).

Hagar, Sarah's handmaid who was sent to sleep with Abraham and conceived a child, evidently was single (Gen. 16:1–16; 21:9–21).

Dinah, who was sexually abused by Shechem, was single (Gen. 34:1–4).

Miriam, sister of Moses and a leader of the Hebrews, was apparently single (Exod. 2:4; 15:20–21; Num. 26:59). Although one tradition asserts that Miriam was married to Hur, Scripture does not support this.

Naomi, whose husband, Elimelech, died, became single again as a widow (Ruth 1:1–5).

Vashti, who opted for divorce rather than disgrace, became single again (Esther 1:1–2:1).

Isaac was single until age forty, which was extremely unusual in Old Testament days (Gen. 24–25).

The variety of biblical patterns and examples of singleness in the Old and New Testaments certainly warrants the theme of this chapter. There are many types of singleness represented, including the never-married, divorced, and widowed persons, and each of these is seen in various situations throughout the entire Bible. Although marriage is normative and usual in both the Old and New Testaments and is seen and understood in the Judeo-Christian heritage, there certainly is a place of prominence for the single person, especially the one having the gift of singleness. The fact that such notable and influential leaders as *Paul, Jeremiah, Ezekiel, John the Baptist, and Jesus were single* speaks highly of the single status and that singleness should be seen as a viable, credible option in society, and especially in Christendom today.

A Philosophy of Ministry to and with Single Adults

Objectives

1. Summarize the attitudes concerning singleness that have existed and progressively changed in the church.
2. Illustrate and describe the attitudes toward singleness in the United States over the last one hundred years.
3. Indicate how demographics demonstrate the need for ministry to single adults.
4. Explain why issues and needs motivate the necessity for ministry to single adults.
5. Assess the ministry potential of single adults.
6. Demonstrate why the life of Jesus validates ministry to single adults.

The Value System: Single Adults in a World of Married Adults

There is pressure in the church today, and to some extent in society, to find the "right person" and marry at a fairly young age.

Almost everywhere we look we see couples. The common American dream of growing up, graduating from high school, going on to college, marrying, raising 2.5 children, owning a house, and living happily ever after still exists in the U.S., but it has lost some of its normalcy.

Older adults tend to have a more traditional attitude of believing a person ought to marry while he or she is young. The *builder* generation (born 1928–1945), for example, expected to marry and begin having children during their early twenties. This traditional attitude of marrying early in life may still be seen and heard in some church foyers across the country. Questions and comments such as, "Why isn't a nice young man like you married yet?" and, "I don't understand how a beautiful girl such as yourself, with a good job, isn't dating," are expressed by well-meaning individuals who are usually unaware of the pressure and discomfort they cause. These remarks, coupled with the seemingly spiritual attitude of "God has someone for you," and "Wait for the perfect person," lay guilt on the young adult who may not feel the need or desire to marry yet.

In the last several decades, however, marital patterns have begun to change and have created a new single adult subculture. These changes have brought new thoughts, attitudes, myths, and sometimes misunderstandings about singleness. For example, the *buster* or postmodern person (born 1965–1982) does not necessarily think the way *builders* do about marriage. Issues like finishing college or grad school, getting a good start on a successful career, or taking time to improve their skills might take precedence over the desire for a permanent relationship. Or the postmodern person may for many years not see a need for marriage at all, believing that the benefits of marriage (sex, children, companionship, etc.) are available without the legal process and formal marriage commitment.

Historical Attitudes Concerning Singleness

Over the course of history single adults have only comprised 2 to 3 percent of the adult population. Marriage was the norm and the expectation of almost all adults. It has only been since the early

1900s that the awareness of single adults has increased and attitudes have changed. A brief overview of the attitudes toward single adults during these years reveals the following information:

- During the first three decades of the twentieth century, single women were labeled *old maids*.
- During the 1930s and 1940s, single women were labeled *spinsters*. Carolyn Koons states: "Society tried to attack the 'problem' of female singleness (seldom were single men focused on) by writing major articles addressing the issue. Some of these included, 'Does It Hurt to Be an Old Maid?' 'Alarming Increase of Old Maids and Bachelors in New England,' 'Family Parasites: The Economic Value of the Unmarried Sister,' 'The Sorrowful Maiden and the Jovial Bachelor,' and 'There Is No Place in Heaven for Old Maids.'"[1]
- During the 1950s and 1960s there was an increase in divorce in the United States. This was the beginning of the institution of "no fault divorce," a legally convenient way to end a marriage without a good (or at least biblical) reason. The reason given for this type of divorce, which all states now have, is termed either "irreconcilable differences" or the marriage is "irretrievably broken." Articles written then seemed to have a questioning bent. Examples included, "When Being Single Stops Being Fun," "How to Be Human Though Single," and "Six Ways to Meet a Man."
- During the 1970s single adults were labeled "swinging singles" thanks to the "new morality" that emerged. The current writings seemed to foster and reflect a more assertive single adult lifestyle. Examples of these included, "What Women Should Know about Single Men," "Humanizing the Meat Market," and "Celebrate Singleness: Marriage May Be Second Best."
- During the 1980s it appeared that singleness was here to stay. The image of "growing single adults" emerged (hard workers, healthy, physically active, affluent, etc.). The 2 or 3 percent minority of singleness was dramatically growing as the percentage of single adults in the nation continued to rise.

Principles for a Philosophy of Ministry

I would like to offer four principles or reasons for targeted ministry to and with single and single-again adults that have emerged over my years of dedicated, continuous involvement in single adult ministry.

1. The demographics demonstrate the need for this ministry.

The following six tables give a clear, concise picture of the numbers, types, and growth of percentage of single adults in our nation. The Census Bureau counts adults as fifteen and older because some states allow marriage at age fifteen. Of all adults age fifteen and older, 43.3 percent were either single or single again in 2000 (see table 1).[2] This does not include the separated people who are actually living as single adults. As shown in table 2, the median age of people entering their first marriage has continued to rise over the last forty years.[3] And as shown in table 3, the growth of single-person households continues to rise.[4]

The percentage of all adults who are married is decreasing. In 1970, 72 percent of all adults in the country were married. By the year 2000 the percentage had decreased to only 56 percent of all adults.[5] Furthermore, the marriage rate dipped 43 percent in the past four decades, from 87.5 marriages per 1,000 unmarried women in 1960, to 49.7 marriages in 1996, leaving it at its lowest point in recorded history.[6] Reasons for this could include:

1. Difficulty in finding a mate
2. Choosing to remain single longer
3. An increase in cohabitation (see below)
4. Creation of the no fault divorce during these years
5. Choosing the single life permanently
6. A possible lowered estimation of marriage in society's eyes
7. Hesitation and reluctance to marry due to the high rate of divorce

Table 1   Percent of all adults who were single or single again in 2000

Never married	59,913,370	27% of all adults
Divorced	21,560,938	9.7% of all adults
Widowed	14,644,500	6.6% of all adults
Total	**96,118,808**	**43.3% of all adults**

Table 2   Median age at first marriage

Year	Men	Women
2000	27.0	25.0
1990	26.1	23.9
1980	24.7	22.0
1970	23.2	20.8
1960	22.8	20.3

Table 3   Single-person households

Year	Percentage of single households
1900	5
1960	13
2000	26

Other single adults are living with friends, parents, relatives, and in rest homes or other such living situations.

The divorce rate continues to soar with each decade, as shown by table 4.[7] Also, the average duration of a first marriage that ends in divorce is eight years, but the average duration of a second marriage that ends in divorce is only six years.[8]

Table 4   Number of divorced adults

1960	3.9 million people living were divorced
1970	4.3 million people living were divorced
1980	9.9 million people living were divorced
1990	15.1 million people living were divorced
2000	20.2 million people living were divorced

The domino effect of divorce is seen in the following statistics, which show that the chance of divorce increases with each additional divorce and remarriage.[9]

41% of first marriages end in divorce.
60% of second marriages end in divorce.
73% of third marriages end in divorce.

For remarriages with children, the divorce rates are very similar.

43% of first marriages divorce.
60% of remarriages with children divorce.
65% remarriages with children from a prior marriage divorce.
65% of simple stepfamilies (1 partner with a child) divorce.
70% of complex stepfamilies (both partners have children) divorce.[10]

In 1970 the divorce rate was 35 people out of 1,000. In 1999 the rate was 250 people out of 1,000.[11] This represents a 680 percent increase! According to Barna's surveys, one fourth of all adults in our nation report having been through at least one divorce. Along with the pains of divorce come many kinds of adjustments, fears, and relational, emotional, financial, and spiritual problems that deserve specialized ministry. Many churches have divorce recovery workshops to address this need (see chapter 5).

Rick Cole, senior pastor of Capitol Christian Center in Sacramento, California, emphasizes the importance of ministry to the divorced: "I see two specific reasons to minister to single adults. One, many are hurting from the pain of divorce and need the love and care the church can provide. The church should be the place to turn to for healing and restoration. Two, many singles are poised to serve in various ministries of the church. They are gifted and hungry to make their lives count. We can release them into ministry to fulfill the call of God."[12]

George Barna relates the skyrocketing growth of single-parent families between 1970 and 2000.[13] In 1900, fewer than 1 of every 100 adults was a single parent of a child under 18. Today, about 6 percent

Table 5 Percentage of all family types that were single-parent families

1970	one ninth were single-parent families
2000	one third were single-parent families

of all adults (6 of every 100) are single parents, roughly 1 of every 3 families! That total has tripled since 1970. Twenty-eight percent of children in the U.S. presently live with just one of their birth parents.

The increase of single-parent families compared to married couples between the years of 1970 and 1999 revealed astonishing figures.[14] The number of *female-headed single-parent families* in 1970 was only 5.5 million, but by 1999 that number had risen to 12.2 million, representing a 122 percent increase. Similarly, the number of *male-headed single-parent families* in 1970 was 1.2 million but by 1999 had risen to 3.2 million, representing a 163 percent increase. It is interesting to note that the number of *married couples* during this same time period only increased 20 percent from 44.7 million to 53.7 million.

Another group that should be included in a single adult ministry are those who face the reality of singleness caused by the death of a spouse. Consider the following facts:

1. There are more widowed people in the U.S. than the entire population of more than four dozen nations of the world, including Belgium, Bolivia, the Czech Republic, Denmark, Ecuador, Greece, Guatemala, Hungary, Ireland, Israel, New Zealand, Norway, Portugal, and Sweden.[15]
2. 17 percent of adults who are sixty-five to sixty-nine years old, 26 percent of those seventy to seventy-four, and 46 percent of those seventy-five or older are widowed.[16]
3. 45 percent of all women sixty-five or older are widowed.[17]
4. 70 percent of all widowed adults live alone.[18]
5. In the next thirty years the U.S. will experience a doubling of the population age sixty-five or older. Implication: a dramatic increase in the number of widowed adults.[19]

The acceptance and increase of cohabitation also has an impact on single adult ministry. *Cohabitation* can be defined as "two unmarried people of the opposite sex in a romantic relationship living together."

A Philosophy of Ministry to and with Single Adults

Table 6 Cohabitation

Year	Number of Couples Cohabiting
2000	5,500,000
1998	4,236,000
1997	4,000,000
1995	3,700,000
1990	2,856,000
1980	1,589,000
1970	523,000
1960	439,000

It is a halfway house for people who do not want the degree of personal, legal, and social commitment that marriage represents. As shown in table 6, cohabitation has skyrocketed 1,150 percent from 1960 to 2000.[20]

To better understand the increase of cohabitation, consider the following facts:

1. Unmarried partner households increased 71 percent during the years 1990–2000.[21]
2. Married couple households only increased 7 percent during the years 1990–2000.[22]
3. The marriage rate dipped 43 percent in the past four decades, from 87.5 marriages per 1,000 unmarried women in 1960 to 49.7 marriages in 1996, leaving it at its lowest point in recorded history.[23]
4. Nearly half of people between ages twenty-five and forty have at some point set up a joint household with a member of the opposite sex outside of marriage.[24]
5. One in three U.S. women choose to live with their partners before marriage, compared to one in ten in the 1950s.[25]
6. Nearly 50 percent of those in their twenties and thirties cohabitate.[26]
7. Half of currently married stepfamilies with children began with cohabitation.[27]

2. The needs and issues of single adults motivate the need for this ministry.

The current number of 82 million unmarried adults in the U.S. age eighteen and older represents more people than the population of most countries in the world. Imagine a country of 82 million people with no missionary. It would be out of the question! Denominational missions departments would be frantically training as many missionaries as possible to send to that country.

Yet this existing number of single adults represents a huge mission field that is largely untapped in most denominations. Lyle Schaller, a church growth expert, suggests that if a church wants a new mission field, it should reach out to single adults and single-parent families in its community.[28] Only 15 percent of all single adults of any age attend any church in the U.S.[29] This enormous group of individuals, many without time-consuming family responsibilities, lies grossly untargeted, unchallenged, unused, undeveloped, and unsaved! The church in North America is, for the most part, missing ministry opportunities to this vast group of people.

The priority of our churches seems to be on marriage and family ministries. As a married man with children, I certainly am not against this. We need to strengthen and minister to marriages and families. There is no doubt about it. This should not be done, however, at the expense or neglect of single and single-again people. One leader states his perspective on this issue by saying, "Every group in the church has unique needs and gifts . . . children, youth, men, women, marrieds, etc. Because we have put emphasis on these groups for so long, we have inadvertently forgotten the single adults and have led them to believe we don't expect them to be involved in ministry. The apostle Paul said that for ministry it is better to be single! (1 Cor. 7:25–35). The purpose of ministry to singles is to help them see they *are* the church and to help them come to a place of ministry."[30]

This minister understands the need for making ministry to single adults one of the church's priorities. Unfortunately, I believe this not to be the case in most of our churches for one or more of the following reasons:

- Most of our pastors across the country are married, and because of doctrine concerning divorce and remarriage, there are few credentialed, remarried pastors.
- Most church board members are married, and usually only once, making it difficult to see this ministry as a priority.
- Most church pastors have not personally experienced the death of their spouse or death of their marriage through divorce and, therefore, do not see this ministry as a priority.
- The aforementioned emphasis and priority on family to the exclusion of single adults is common in U.S. churches.
- The "traditional ministries" (children, youth, music, etc.) receive the priority in the church budget.
- A lack of understanding of the unique issues and needs of single adults is another reason (see chapter 4). Many leaders have not consistently worked with separated, divorced, or widowed persons, and therefore, the needs of these individuals are not at the forefront of their minds (see chapter 3).
- Most pastors lack an understanding of the benefits a targeted ministry to single adults can bring to the church.
- There are a myriad of myths and misunderstandings about single adults that church leaders and married adults believe (see chapter 3).
- Many pastors are unwilling or reluctant to deal with the difficult issues that many single and single-again people have, and hesitate to take care of additional needy people.

Single adults need and deserve the opportunities of salvation and spiritual growth as much as married adults do. Because of the previously stated reasons, however, many single adults do not feel a part of and are not retained in our *family-oriented* churches. It is my contention that many unmarried adults need specialized ministry opportunities to reach, retain, and disciple them before they will be integrated into and involved in the total life of the church, which is the ultimate goal of ministry to single adults. The experience of many single adult pastors and leaders who have ministered to single adults underscores this.

Scott Nelson, former single adult/young adult pastor at First Assembly in Fort Wayne, Indiana, relates his perspective concerning this.

> How many times have you heard a pastor say from the pulpit something like "turn to your spouse and say . . ." or "any guy who says he doesn't struggle with this (could be any issue) is lying, just ask his wife"? I cringe every time I hear these kinds of insensitive statements because I know we have a large number of single adults in our congregation. Some of them are still hurting from the pain of divorce, others are grieving a lost loved one and still others are reminded of that old familiar ache in their heart that represents a desire to be married. When it comes to the issues that single adults face in real life, we, the church, are at best insensitive and, at worst, downright ignorant.
>
> The mission of the church is to win the lost and make disciples. Statistics indicate that about 45% of our adult population in the U.S. is unmarried. The obvious question to ask ourselves is, "does 45% of my church consist of unmarried people?" If not, then perhaps we are overlooking a huge and growing mission field.[31]

3. The ministry potential of single adults authenticates the need for this ministry.

This huge, vastly unreached group of single adults could literally affect and change the spiritual dryness and emptiness of our nation. Imagine hundreds of thousands of single and single-again adults, many not having the time, energy, and financial constraints of a family, passionate for Christ and his church! Imagine if even 50 percent of our churches were deliberately recognizing, reaching, restoring, discipling, and releasing single adults into the kingdom for effective ministry! A high percentage of these individuals would be without children and would have distinct advantages over married adults (with and without children) in at least three categories:

1. *Use of time*—Single adults have total control over their time. They do not need to be concerned with how their activities affect another person's schedule, as married adults do. Their time is their own to use as they wish. For example, if a single

individual has the desire to be a part of a short-term missions trip, he or she does not need to check with a spouse to be gone for a period of time.

2. *Making decisions*—Single adults also have total control over the many and varied decisions that need to be made. They do not need to ask a spouse's opinion concerning their choices. Using the same example of the missions trip, the decision to go could be made without having to consult or gain permission or concession from a spouse.

3. *Use of money*—Single adults have total control over the management of their money and do not have to consult a spouse regarding its use. The choice to spend money to go on a missions trip would not have to be negotiated with a spouse.

I have had the privilege of organizing, training, and leading seven missions teams to other countries on short-term ministry trips. I can speak from experience on these issues because each team was comprised of single adults. Single adults have gifts, abilities, resources, time, and a desire and passion to be used of God (often without the constraints married adults have). The church needs to understand and embrace this largely untapped resource group of people. I wonder what the results would show if a survey were taken in every church across the nation comparing the percentage of single adults and married adults *attending the church* with the percentage of single adults and married adults *involved in ministry* anywhere in the church. The results might be surprising.

Additionally, those in leadership understand that a person involved in ministry grows much faster spiritually and relationally than one who is not. Considering the shortness of time before Christ's return, it is imperative for the church to maximize its assistance to individuals in their process of spiritual growth.

4. The life of Jesus validates the need for this ministry.

The greatest single adult who ever lived, Jesus, proved the ministry effectiveness a single adult could have by living and modeling his life in service to his Father and to humankind. Jesus said,

"For even the Son of Man did not come to be served, but to serve" (Mark 10:45). His example of consistent, passionate, selfless ministry provides tremendous inspiration to single adults and their leaders around the world. Would it have been possible for Jesus to keep the schedule he kept had he been married? Would a spouse have put up with his extensive travel? Would his diverse ministry activities have been possible had he had a wife? Would as many of the demands of the crowds and the crying needs of individuals have been met had Jesus been married and had to also attend to his spouse's needs?

And consider his death—Jesus knew what crucifixions were like. They were common in his day; he had seen them before. Had he been married, would his spouse have been able to bear the excruciating, impending death of her husband? It may have been his Father's plan for Jesus to remain single while on the earth to more effectively carry out his divine will. God knew the extra concerns and anxieties that came with marriage and, knowing the difficult plan for his Son, may not have wanted to encumber Jesus with additional responsibilities.

Jesus's passionate ministry life certainly exhibits a model for single adults to follow. Not that they should remain single all their lives; many, if not most, will marry at some point. During singleness, however, the life of Jesus is the example to be emulated and imitated. Jesus was the greatest single adult who ever lived. His life validates the need for ministry to and with single adults.

Practical Principles to Help a Church Minister to and with Single Adults

Objectives

1. Demonstrate why the five types of single adults desire and need to be in a family.
2. Illustrate the practical and scriptural reasons for "family-ing" single adults.
3. Discuss why a church may need to redefine and expand its mission to accommodate and minister to single adults.
4. Examine why a church may need to expand its definition of *family*.
5. Show why a church may need to rethink its biblical and theological roots and develop a new perspective on singleness.
6. List and discuss several prominent myths that exist in the church today concerning singleness and single adults.

The Need to Be in a Family

Single adults need the spiritual instruction, spiritual and relational involvement, and community that the church can and should provide as much as or perhaps more than married adults do. They have a need to be connected to and become part of a *family*. This need may become apparent in a church if some single adults are vocal about this desire. But if it does not surface, that does not mean the desire for family is not there. Silence does not negate the need. This need for connection to and inclusion in a family is especially true because of the various causes of singleness and resulting lifestyles that are common. All single adults lack a marital partner to share the hopes, hurts, decisions, and joys of life. Consider the following:

1. *Young, never-married*—These adults are transitioning from the home(s) of their parent(s). Some are not physically or relationally close to their family and crave, deserve, and need the closeness of a church family and the personal direction that can result from being connected to a church body.

2. *Divorced*—These adults have experienced a tragic break of a marriage, many times with children. Their family has been torn apart, whether by their desire, their spouse's, or mutual consent. They need the acceptance, community, and nonjudgmental love a church family can provide.

3. *Separated*—These adults are in limbo, not knowing how to reconcile with their spouse, and possibly not desiring to do so. They may feel lonely, isolated, confused, hurt, and frustrated, and they may lack direction for their life as a result of a spouse's or their own leaving. They are legally married but living a single lifestyle and desperately need the acceptance and unconditional love a church family can provide.

4. *Widowed*—These adults have lost their spouse to death by no choice of their own. They may feel helplessly alone and lost, not knowing how to feel about themselves and their identity now that their spouse is gone. They may also feel abandoned by God, not knowing why he allowed their loved one to die. They feel they are still married, but they are actually living as a single adult, although they do not

wish to acknowledge this for quite a while. They need the attention, understanding, care, and "family feel" the church can provide.

5. *Single parents*—These adults have become single parents by chance, change, or choice, whether theirs or someone else's. They may experience loneliness, frustration over lack of finances, difficulty rearing children alone, confusion, pain over loss of a spouse, a desire for adult conversation, etc. They have one of the toughest tasks in the world! They try to take on the role and tasks two parents may have previously filled. In my opinion these families are many of today's orphans and widows. They need the unconditional love, stability, provision of financial help, time away from children, and many other things that a church family willing to get involved can provide.

It is evident that all of these single adults and their children not only need *to be in a family* but desperately need *to be "family-ed."* The word *family* is usually thought of and used as a noun. The "biological family," "the family of God," and similar expressions are common examples of this use. However, the word *family* is more than a noun. It is also a verb! The New Testament encourages Christians and the church to "family" each other. The Scripture exhorts us to care for each other; this certainly includes the single parent and children who are fatherless:

God setteth the solitary in families.

Psalm 68:6 KJV

And whoever welcomes a little child like this in my name welcomes me.

Matthew 18:5

Religion that God our Father accepts as pure and faultless is this: to look after orphans and widows.

James 1:27

But you, O God, . . . are the helper of the fatherless.

Psalm 10:14

For in you the fatherless find compassion.

Hosea 14:3

God's Word challenges us to be our brother's keeper. It is time for the church to wake up and see the desperate needs and desires of single parents and their families! It is time for us to accept, love, and minister to them unconditionally—to family them. Practical needs of single parents that the church could provide include: auto repairs, home repairs, child care, the opportunity to be away from the kids to be with other adults, financial help to attend a retreat or pay bills, Christmas gifts for the children, and on and on. Adults in a first marriage may not see or understand these needs of the single-parent family as easily as parents in blended or stepfamilies. Remarried adults, having been single themselves, are usually more aware of, have empathy for, and become involved with helping single-parent families.

Just as the single-parent family needs to be cared for, single adults want and need the family atmosphere and the caring and benefits that people in a loving church can give. Sharing meals, spending time together during holidays, and including single adults in other group events are just a few ways individuals can minister to single adults. Single adults want to be included in a family, and frankly, they also have much to offer nuclear, blended, expanded, grandparent, and other types of families. The church is the vehicle God has ordained to family those who have no family or do not have one physically or emotionally close enough to enjoy.

Practical Principles for Single Adult Ministry

I believe for the local church to effectively minister to single adults today, there are several principles that may need to be discussed, resolved, and implemented by the church leaders.

The church may need to redefine and expand its mission.

Based on my thirty-one years of experience with hundreds of churches with and without single adult ministries, I believe the majority of evangelical churches in most denominational churches in the U.S., as well as most independent churches, are mainly *marriage and family focused*. Pastors and church leaders are usually more concerned with reaching families, especially the nuclear family, than with reaching single adults. As stated in chapter 2, the principle of reaching families should continue, but it needs to be redefined and expanded to include the five types of single adults who do not always comfortably fit in churches that emphasize and promote with phrases like "the family church" and "family night" or that have an abundance of "marriage classes" and "family classes."

Harold Ivan Smith, a prolific writer and speaker for thirty years to and for the single adult community, says, "Any church that ignores single adults is signing its death warrant! That sounds like a rather strong and opinionated statement. Yet, what else can we say to those churches who treat single adult ministry as only a fad to replace their former fascination with bus ministry?"[1] He suggests five excellent reasons why a church cannot ignore single adults.

1. A church that ignores single adults fails to underwrite tomorrow's leadership.

Thousands of skilled, competent, passionate adults are only pew-warmers. This is not because they are unwilling to serve but because many times church leadership thinks young adults should either "grow up" or "settle down and get married" before they are mature enough or eligible to be in key leadership positions. Sadly, it is also true that many church leaders and pastors look for married couples before single adults to fill important leadership roles in the church. It is as though there is something more normal, mature, or spiritual about being married.

2. A church that ignores single adults fails to appreciate the pattern demonstrated by the early church in Acts 6.

In Acts 6:1–7 the church responds to the needs of the widowed, or *chera* (those without a mate). Remember that James wrote, "Religion that God our Father accepts as pure and faultless is this: to look after orphans and widows in their distress" (James 1:27). The weight of the Old Testament thought is summarized in severe curses on anyone who takes advantage of the *chera* (Exod. 22:22).

3. A church that ignores single adults fails to follow Jesus's example.

The words of Jesus on the cross to John were, "Here is your mother" (John 19:27). These words expressed one of the Father's priorities—to take care of a widow in her grief who was now losing her son. If Christ took time while dying to remember the needs of a widow, how much more should the church take care of those without a mate?

4. A church that ignores single adults is a slave to the past rather than a previewer of the future.

There is a sense, today, of the church hoping that the majority of society will return to the days of the nuclear family—with an original husband, wife, and two or three children. The church is "in exile" from the days of the nuclear family we so fondly remember and imagine. I personally believe, as Harold Ivan Smith says, "The church must painfully abandon some of its most cherished myths and cultural notions concerning the family in order to embrace the realities of twenty-first century (and beyond) living."[2] Societal practices and trends have clearly shown that this "how it used to be" norm is no longer the case, nor will it be in the future. Smith continues, "I believe singleness to be the permanent direction of the American population, not because of some post-Vietnam or post-Watergate consequences, but because the drift of American culture for more than 200 years has clearly been in this direction."[3]

It is time the church sees the "singling of America" as an *opportunity to be seized* rather than only a problem to be solved! It is time to turn what looks bad into something good. It is time to train the church to teach single adults to become "kingdom seekers rather than mate seekers."

5. A church that ministers to and with single adults will help them mature, make spiritual commitments, and establish kingdom priorities that will lead them into better marriages.

I firmly believe this to be so. A church that targets single adults for ministry to and with them will help build stronger individuals for Christ, from both a redemptive and preventative perspective. Effective single adult ministries can and will help prevent future divorces because of the individual healing and training that takes place in such ministries. The spiritual and relational growth that results in people is invaluable, and it is uniquely brought about by the sharing of people with similar circumstances.

Greg Davis states, "Because of common experiences there is a greater understanding of the struggles as well as help and encouragement. People without common experiences may be able to sympathize, feel *for* you, but cannot empathize, feel *with* you, because they do not have similar experiences (2 Cor. 1:4). Because of this commonality, there is a dynamic that fosters spiritual, emotional and relational growth."[4]

Helen Marispini explains the benefits of a single adult ministry group by saying, "Being a part of the single adult ministry has given me a place where I can come and find friendship, encouragement and support. My friends hold me accountable to my commitment to the Lord as we share in each other's lives."[5]

The church may need to expand its traditional or normal definition of **family** *to include and minister to at least ten types of families in society today.*

We must become the family God intended us to be—*the family of God*. Chapter 2 showed some of the changing demographics in our nation, providing some statistical understanding of the creation of these families. Today's family households reveal these types:

1. *Nuclear family*—an original husband and wife living together and rearing their children.
2. *Single-parent family*—a never-married, divorced, or widowed parent with his or her own or someone else's children (step, foster, or adopted).
3. *Stepparent family*—a parent rearing his or her biological, foster, or adopted children and marrying (hopefully) and living with another adult.

4. *Blended family*—two adults and their biological, step, foster, or adopted children from two previous families marrying (hopefully) and living together.
5. *Single adult family*—one or more single adult(s) of the same or opposite sex living by himself or herself or together in a platonic or romantic relationship.
6. *Grandparent family*—one or more grandparents rearing their children's biological, step, foster, or adopted children.
7. *Separated family*—two parents who are separated (possibly legally) but not legally divorced from each other, rearing their own biological, step, adopted, or foster children.
8. *Homosexual parent(s)/partner(s) family*—two adults, one or both living in the homosexual lifestyle and rearing children (whether biological, adopted, step, foster in some states, by surrogate, or by artificial insemination).
9. *Homosexual/Heterosexual parent(s)/partner(s) family*—these adults stay married because they emotionally love each other and may have children from the same sources as the previous family type. This family is more likely to occur in conservative churches where the homosexual spouse might be economically harmed by coming out.
10. *Expanded family*—any of these family types taking in a child from the court and rearing him or her for a temporary period of time.

Most of these ten family types are in almost every church in our country. Due to many variables, however, larger churches increase the likelihood of higher percentages of the last nine family types. It should also be noted that the challenges for the nuclear family may not be nearly as vast and compounded as the other types. Imagine the possible confusion and complications in a family whose parent(s) or children find themselves in or from more than one family type! The combinations, complexities, and resulting issues of today's family are astounding, and they make the need for godly wisdom extremely important (James 1:5). Without wisdom resulting in effective ministry, we will not become the family God intended us to be—the family of God!

The church may need to rethink its biblical and theological roots and develop a new perspective on singleness.[6]

Chapter 1 discussed the many examples of singleness in both the Old and New Testaments. Although singleness was the exception in Old Testament cultures, it clearly existed, and God certainly used many single adults as mighty influencers to proclaim his message (Jeremiah, Ezekiel, Hosea, Deborah, Hagar, Dinah, Miriam, Naomi, and Vashti). The New Testament brought a new emphasis on and recognition to singleness as a viable option for ministry as shown by the writings of Paul in 1 Corinthians 7:7–8 and the words of Jesus in Matthew 19:11–12, where the "gift of singleness" is mentioned. Certainly Paul, John the Baptist, Anna, Mary, Martha, Lydia, Titus, Timothy, Mary Magdalene, and most of all, Jesus were effective ministers as single adults. Paul's opinion of having more flexibility and less anxiety as a single adult than a married adult (1 Cor. 7:32–33) should possibly be given more credit and carry more influence in the church today than it currently does.

The church needs to help people reject many false, cruel myths and stereotypes about singleness to become the community of healing, strength, help, and wholeness God intends it to be.

These myths stem from many sources (pastors, married adults, single adults, society in general), and they tend to foster an unfair, negative image of the single lifestyle. The following myths are some of the more common ones.

Single adults are lonely.

Because marriage has been considered the norm in our culture, and especially in the church, it has also been perceived as the romantic goal to achieve. Singleness is often thought of as a passing phase to be resolved by the ultimate state of marriage, so consequently, single adults must be lonely! I am quick to point out that there are some lonely aspects of singleness, and single adults do get lonely sometimes. It does not take being single, however, to be lonely. There are also countless lonely married adults in the U.S. Many married men and women are lying eighteen inches away from their spouse in bed but are miles apart in their relationship.

Single adults want to get married.

This attitude is perpetuated by well-meaning married adults who wonder and sometimes ask why many single adults have not yet married. One of my pet peeves involves the phrase, "I want you to meet my better half." Married people are not two halves coming together to make a whole! Single adults are not half people until they are married! There are many married adults who do not exhibit wholeness, and there are many single adults who do. It is true that most single adults do want to someday marry, but there are also some who are not looking to marry. We must emphasize wholeness in Christ, not marriage. Colossians 2:10 says, "Ye are complete in him" (KJV); "You have been given fullness in Christ" (NIV).

Single men are irresponsible.

Society has a tendency to label people who do not conform to its expectations as irresponsible. Carolyn Koons addresses this by saying, "A few studies have attempted to indicate that the thirty-nine-year-old single male group is one of the most irresponsible segments of society (highest crime rate, arrest rate, drug rate, entrance into mental institutions). But the 1980s provided a whole new perspective on male singleness. Since then, young, educated single men have been running major companies. Singleness offers men a time of freedom for education and career. . . . Men are more apt to take their time to wait for just the right woman to spend their lives with."[7]

Single adults are sexually frustrated.

Although it is true that some single adults may be sexually frustrated, especially the widowed and divorced who may have had sex in marriage on a regular basis, it is also true that there are single adults who are abstinent, are well adjusted to singleness, and are aware of the confusion and dangers that exist with an active sexual life outside of a lifetime commitment. It also should be noted that marriage does not preclude sexual frustration. Pastoral counseling has revealed many married adults, Christian and non-Christian, who are not sexually fulfilled.

Single adults have fewer problems than married adults.

Nothing could be further from the truth! Single adults, in fact, may have more problems than married adults due to the lack of a partner to assist them with the daily responsibilities of home care, auto care, children's issues, family issues, etc. Decisions concerning everyday living are many times made alone, without the help of a dedicated, interested spouse.

Single adults are "on the prowl."

Some think that most single adults are always looking for Mr. or Miss Right. It is true that many single adults want to marry someday, but it is untrue that most are obsessed with finding a mate.

Single adults must be afraid of making a commitment.

Some people think this must be the reason why a thirty-year-old with a good job, church involvement, and seemingly balanced life is not yet married. Many single adults want to make the commitment of marriage but have not found the right person to commit to. It is also true that some are not yet married because it is not God's timing in their life to be married. I believe God's desire for single adults concerning marriage includes not only the right person but the right reasons and right timing.

Single adults have more time than married adults.

Some married adults think a person without a spouse has more time to spend on himself or herself. Although it is true that a single adult does not have to spend time meeting a spouse's needs and may focus on himself or herself (as stated earlier), it is also true that the many domestic tasks of a household, financial decisions, and other decisions have to be accomplished without the help of a spouse. These responsibilities take more time to fulfill alone than with a spouse's assistance.

Single adults are a threat to married adults.

As a pastor to single adults, I have had more than a few tell me they were neglected, ostracized, or at the least made to feel uncomfortable by married adults because they were perceived as a threat. This attitude would surface in a wife subtly indicating fear that an attractive single woman might interest her husband or a husband showing jealousy or reluctance about a single man getting too close to his wife. This threat, however, is almost never the intention of the single adult. It is usually caused by insecurity in the married person.

Single adults are not complete until they are married.

This stems from the belief that everyone should get married. It is a myth probably believed by more seniors and builders (born 1928–1946, usually more traditional, conservative adults) and some boomers (born 1946–1964) than by busters (born 1965–1983) and "millenials" or "Y'ers" (born 1984–2000), who are younger and usually more nontraditional. In general, the church still views marriage as the normal, usual, ultimately fulfilling lifestyle and believes that all, or most, adults should enter it sometime early into adulthood.

The expectation of producing children also accompanies marriage. It is precisely this marriage and family emphasis in most evangelical churches, without an open acceptance and emphasis on singleness, that tends to alienate or, at the very least, cause some single adults to feel uncomfortable and sometimes question their completeness. Marriage certainly does not ensure completeness. Only Christ ensures and brings completeness to a person!

Single adults have more money than married adults.

It is often assumed that because a person does not have a spouse they have more money to spend on themselves than one who is married. This is only true for the small percentage of single adults who have a high salary. Probably most single adults have a lower standard of living than married adults because:

- They have only one income but all the same living costs as a two-person household (a married couple may have two incomes).
- A divorce causes loss of one salary, child support costs, possible moving costs, possibly a lower paying job due to schedule changes, additional child care costs, spousal support costs, attorney costs, and so forth.
- A death of a spouse causes loss of one salary and may force the widowed adult to live on a fixed income.
- Single parents may raise children alone with little or no consistent financial child support from the other parent. Studies have shown:
  a. More than five million custodial parents were without awards of financial support from their child(ren)'s other parent.[8]
  b. Only 67 percent of mothers due payments receive at least a portion of the amount owed.[9]
  c. The average amount of child support received by these parents was $3,600.[10]
- Extra repair expenses may arise due to not having a spouse to make light auto repairs, do household repairs, mend clothes, clean the house, etc.

There are other myths about single adults also. Some of these include:

- Single adults are "wild swingers" (whatever that means!).
- Single adults don't understand family life.
- Single adults are selfish and set in their ways.

Many of these myths could be applied to married adults too! Irresponsibility, not understanding family life, selfishness, being set in your ways, feeling incomplete, being a threat to another's marriage, sexual frustration, or loneliness are a part of many marriages across this country. Singleness does not have a corner on any of these traits.

It is clear the church has a tremendous opportunity to minister to single adults of all types. It is also abundantly clear that many churches may have to adjust attitudes, become more open-minded, become more educated about the needs, desires, and issues of single adults, and become more intentional about accepting, reaching, and "family-ing" single adults. The opportunity to minister to millions of single adults in the U.S. *needs to be realized, understood, and seized*! The opportunity to build the local church by reaching single adults and their families *needs to be grasped*! The opportunity to bring the message of hope and wholeness to the largest untapped people group in our country *needs to be acted upon*!

PART
TWO

Overview of Single
Adult Ministry

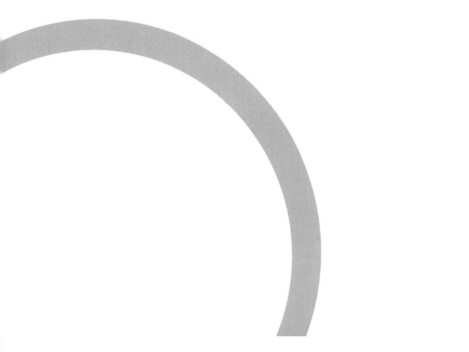

Ministry today is much different than it was in the 1960s and 1970s. Mass communication, mass media, high-tech tools, and other means of spreading the message of Christ have enabled a much broader and quicker approach to evangelism.

These changes in spreading the gospel, however, are not the only ones facing the church. Society as a whole and people as individuals have become much more complex, diverse, and unique, making ministry more complicated and complex than it used to be. The once familiar, predominant, and traditional biblical example of family, the *nuclear family* with its original husband and wife and their biological children, has been eroded, abused, and changed. As explained in chapter 3, the word *family* now includes at least ten types of units prevalent in our culture today: the nuclear family, single parent family, stepparent family, blended family, grandparent family, separated family, single adult family, homosexual parents/partners family, homosexual/heterosexual parents/partners family, and the expanded family (see chapter 3 for definitions of these).

These family types were addressed in chapter 3. It is interesting to note that *all of these types of families contain, or may contain, an adult who was or is single or single-again.* Think about it. The single-parent family is definitely led by a single adult. The stepparent family contains at least one parent who, for one of many reasons, was a single parent. The blended family contains two parents who were single parents. The grandparent family could be led by a single adult. The separated family contains two parents who are legally married but, in reality, are living a single lifestyle. The single adult family contains one or more single adults of the same or opposite sex living together. The two types of homosexual families contain one or more adults who may be single for one of many reasons. The expanded family could be led by a parent who is single.

It is because of these complex families existing in society and the church today that a targeted ministry to single adults, of at least minimum proportions, needs to be strongly considered and implemented by many churches that are in a unique position to reach them—especially those churches that are midsize or larger or are in or near a midsize or large city. This is where the majority of single adults live. Methods and practices of the 1960s and 1970s will not effectively reach, minister to, and retain today's diversity of people and their various needs.

Objectives of This Section

The following objectives frame the structure of part 2 of this book.

1. *Understand the diverse needs of single adults.* Married and single adults have the *same spiritual needs but different personal needs.* A church that understands the many unique personal needs of the five types of single adults is a church poised to minister to them. Intentional and purposeful ministry is needed to address the varied and diverse issues facing single and single-again individuals. They deserve the opportunity of teaching and discussion from a biblical and single adult perspective. If the church does not address these issues, where are they going to get their information? The answer is obvious: the world, television, movie theater, video store, friends, etc. These sources, however, are usually not very biblical or healthy ones from which to learn.

2. *Help gain a clear understanding of the needs, issues, and life of the five types of single adults in our society and the church today.* Because the evangelical church in our society is so marriage and family focused, single adults often go unnoticed, neglected, and untargeted in Christian circles. Married adults, pastors, parachurch ministry leaders, district church leaders, and national church leaders need to be educated concerning the five types of single and single-again adults that comprise 44 percent of all adults in the United States today. Each of these types of adults has many similar issues, needs, hopes, hurts, talents, and desires. Each of them, however, also has quite different and unique issues, needs, hopes, hurts, talents, and desires. These people are an untapped source of creativity, time, talent, and resources for the kingdom of God. It is time the church understood the vast reservoir of ministry talents these single adults possess!

3. *Identify, recognize, distinguish between, and be able to choose one or more of the ministry models that are right for their particular time and place of ministry to single adults.* There are at least seven distinct models of ministry being used to minister to single adults today. Many ministries choose to begin one model and then add others as vision, resources, and leadership are obtained. Each of these will be listed and described from four perspectives:

> Important elements of the model
> Attracting and retaining people
> Meeting location—on or off the church grounds
> Minimum leadership recommended

4. *Explain the six dimensions of life, compare and contrast them, and conclude how these can be a part of a ministry to single adults.* God created human beings to be multifaceted creatures comprised of at least six dimensions: spiritual, social, mental, physical, relational, and emotional. Each of these areas of life represents certain needs that can, in a large measure, be met by the Lord and his people in and through the ministries of the church:

> *Spiritual*—helping a person develop his or her spirit and relationship with God.
> *Social*—helping a person grow socially and establish healthy relationships with *groups of people*, both males and females.
> *Mental*—helping a person continue learning in a variety of areas that will affect and increase his or her knowledge, wisdom, and understanding.
> *Physical*—helping a person develop physical skills and maintain relatively good physical fitness.
> *Relational*—helping a person establish healthy relationships with individuals of the same and opposite sex.
> *Emotional*—helping a person understand and manage his or her emotions.

5. *List and describe the primary characteristics of a ministry to single adults so a leader could implement them into a ministry. It is also my intention to show four principles a church with a ministry to single adults will learn.* There are many basic traits relevant to

single adult ministry that are advisable to know and understand before embarking on the mission of beginning a ministry. Many of the primary characteristics will be identified and discussed to assist in gaining a concise understanding of them.

A church with an active ministry to single adults will see a higher percentage of single and single-again adults who are active in the total life of the church than if they had not had such a ministry. Succinctly stated, one of the goals of this ministry is to see single adults actively involved in the church and become contributing parts of the body of Christ. As a result of this happening, there are at least four principal truths a congregation will be faced with accepting and learning. These will be presented and discussed in chapter 8.

Understanding the Diverse Needs of Single Adults

Objectives

1. Identify the many types of people a single adult ministry will attract.
2. Describe and illustrate the principle of a specific ministry for single adults as an *entry point* into the church.
3. List various needs and issues of each of the five types of single adults.
4. Analyze and demonstrate the responsibility of the church to biblically address these issues of single adults.
5. Examine some of the basic challenges of singleness a church should meet.

God has ordained the local church to build his kingdom, reach the world, and reach and teach individuals—including single adults. The church, however, must learn to understand the common needs single adults have as well as the unique needs single adults of each *age group* and *need group* possess to be able to effectively minister to these needs. The church, by its God-given mandate to love and accept people, will draw all types and backgrounds of people who have diverse issues and needs. A church that has a specific ministry to single adults, however, will be even more likely to draw all types of people, both healthy and unhealthy spiritually, emotionally, and relationally, because the very nature and purpose of this ministry is to accept and love people.

As a former pastor to single adults and young adults, I have seen many spiritually mature single adults come into one of our ministry groups, accept leadership roles, and become dynamic, positive influences on the rest of the group. I refer to these individuals as *lifters*. They lift people spiritually, emotionally, and relationally because they are spiritually and emotionally healthy. There have been countless individuals in ministries who have led effective prayer ministries, discussion groups, Bible studies, special events, workshops, classes, and so forth. Single adults with a passion for the Lord and a variety of organizational skills, artistic abilities, cooking skills, evangelistic passion, counseling skills, and various other leadership skills have proven effective in diverse ministry opportunities. These volunteers have helped lead people to Christ, bring emotional and relational healing to many lives, and bring balance and growth to the ministry.

On the other hand, the fact that some of the people drawn to a single adult ministry are spiritually and emotionally weak and unhealthy is no secret. I refer to these people as *leaners*. They need to lean on others for emotional, relational, and spiritual support and help for a while. The church is one place where they hope to and should receive unconditional love, acceptance, and healing.

Jesus understood this principle. Upon hearing the Pharisees question his actions of eating with the sinners and publicans (Matt. 9:10–13), Jesus said to them, "It is not the healthy who need a doctor, but the sick" (v. 12). His statement was both an indictment and a challenge. The church should be the one place people go to get healed in every way: spiritually, relationally, emotionally, and physically. We desperately need to teach and help people model unconditional love, acceptance, and forgiveness if we are to be the church of reconciliation and healing God intends us to be.

A Wide Variety of People

A single adult ministry attracts all sorts of people. The following list identifies the many types of individuals, healthy and unhealthy, that a church, and especially a single adult ministry, will attract.

1. People who are single for a variety of reasons
   a. divorced
   b. widowed
   c. separated
   d. never married
   e. single parent
2. Handicapped people
   a. physically handicapped
   b. mentally handicapped
   c. socially handicapped
3. Abused people
   a. physically
   b. sexually
   c. verbally
   d. emotionally
   e. psychologically
4. People of various sexual preferences
   a. heterosexuals
   b. homosexuals
   c. bisexuals
   d. transsexuals
   e. transvestites
   f. sexual addicts
5. People of various academic levels
   a. people who dropped out of high school
   b. people with a high school degree
   c. people with an associate's degree
   d. people with a bachelor's degree
   e. people with a master's degree
   f. people with a Ph.D.

6. People of various spiritual levels
   a. spiritually mature people
   b. spiritually immature people
   c. backslidden people
   d. heathen/pagan people
7. People with other issues
   a. poorly groomed
   b. well-groomed
   c. abandoned
   d. family-oriented
   e. family-less
   f. gainfully employed
   g. jobless
   h. homeowners
   i. homeless
   j. cohabiters
   k. convicts
   l. gamblers
   m. prostitutes
   n. drug addicts

This list illustrates the dire need for the church to be a *spiritual hospital* where people can receive help for various issues in their life! The pain, sin, and difficult circumstances people find themselves in require the truth of Psalm 147:3, "He heals the brokenhearted and binds up their wounds." The challenge of this verse is to understand that *many times God heals through us, his church.* We need to be available and willing to *rub shoulders, hands, and hearts* with all these types of people and let Christ accomplish his healing work through us.

The Same Spiritual Needs

Marital status has little to do with spiritual need; single adults have the same spiritual needs as married adults. Our humanness dictates the truth that we all have the same spiritual needs because of our sinful, selfish nature. Whether an unbeliever or believer, married or single, all adults are in the same category concerning our lost condition and need of a Savior. The following list highlights some of the more common spiritual needs of adults that can be anticipated in a single adult ministry.

- salvation
- forgiveness
- water baptism
- Holy Spirit baptism
- obedience
- fellowship
- spiritual gifts
- discipleship
- prayer
- commitment
- Bible teaching
- spiritual growth
- repentance

An Entry Point into the Church

The church, for the most part, is doing an adequate, sometimes excellent job of addressing these needs through preaching, teaching, discussion, small group studies, prayer meetings, etc., *for the adults who are in the church body.* But this is the strategic issue. *Many single adults are not in a church body* because of the lack of an organized opportunity for relationship with other single adults who have interests and issues similar to theirs. Because they are not in the church, they do not have the opportunity to receive the excellent spiritual food that comes through preaching, teaching, discussion, and community to bring them to a relationship with Christ and assist them in their spiritual growth. A targeted ministry for single adults can *attract them and bring them into a loving fellowship of believers.*

As stated in chapter 2, a church that does not have a specific, targeted ministry to one or more of the age groups or need groups usually has a lower percentage of single adults than churches that do have a specialized ministry. A specialized ministry to single adults serves as a *comfortable, identifiable entry point* into the church body for many single adults, especially the single-again person who already may feel let down or misunderstood by the church. As also stated earlier, the need for connection to a church family and the need to experience community is many times greater for single adults than married adults for obvious reasons.

Personal Needs and Issues of Single Adults

Meeting the spiritual needs of individuals is certainly one of the top priorities of most churches across the country. The personal needs, however, should not be overlooked. Dr. Bill Flanagan, former singles pastor and current executive pastor of Newport Presbyterian Church in Newport, California, emphasizes the importance of teaching about and ministering to personal needs. "Single adult ministries that are biblically focused should not be narrowly tuned to spiritual development only, but open to the totality of the human experience."[1]

Table 7 offers a list of personal/topical needs and issues pertaining to the five types of single adults. I have included separated persons, even though they are legally married, because in reality they are living a single life. This table is by no means comprehensive, nor is it meant to imply that every single adult in any particular category has all of these issues in his or her life. It is given as a guide to understand the main, probable issues that can be taught and discussed. More concerning this will be discussed in chapter 5.

It is apparent that many issues listed will relate to all types of single adults, but probably on different levels and to varying degrees. Age and life circumstances greatly affect the degree to which these topics are relevant, and they should be considered when planning teaching opportunities and schedules.

Table 7   Needs and issues of single adults

NEED/ISSUE	Never Married	Divorced	Separated	Widowed	Single Parent
1. Acceptance	x	x	x	x	x
2. **Bitterness**		x	x	x	x
3. **Handling change**	x	x	x	x	x
4. **Giving/receiving forgiveness**	x	x	x	x	x
5. Understanding emotions	x	x	x	x	x
6. **My former spouse**		x	x	x	x
7. **Managing grief**		x	x	x	x
8. Managing anger	x	x	x	x	x
9. **Dating/dating again**	x	x	x	x	x
10. **Relating to the married**	x	x	x	x	x
11. **Premarital education**	x				x
12. **Re-marital education**		x	x	x	x
13. Self-esteem	x	x	x	x	x
14. **Developing identity**	x	x	x	x	x
15. **Accepting singleness**	x	x	x	x	x
16. **Friendships with same or opposite sex**	x	x	x	x	x
17. Managing money	x	x	x	x	x
18. **Single parenting**		x	x	x	x
19. **Setting goals**	x	x	x	x	x
20. Career issues	x	x	x	x	x
21. Learning to risk	x	x	x	x	x
22. Depression		x	x	x	x
23. **Blending families**		x	x	x	x
24. **Divorce recovery**		x	x		x
25. Real/false guilt	x	x	x	x	x
26. **Stepparenting**		x	x	x	x
27. Learning to trust	x	x	x	x	x
28. **Loneliness**	x	x	x	x	x
29. **Sexuality**	x	x	x	x	x
30. Gossip	x	x	x	x	x
31. Jealousy	x	x	x	x	x
32. Hope	x	x	x	x	x
33. **Rejection**	x	x	x		x
34. Stress	x	x	x	x	x
35. Selfishness	x	x	x	x	x
36. **Adjusting to widowhood**				x	x
37. **Divorce and remarriage**		x	x		x

Bold = Issues/topics that need and deserve biblical teaching from a *single adult perspective.*

Some of the personal issues and topics listed are already addressed in churches by pastors and teachers, and the instruction relates equally well to married or single adults. The issues and topics in bold type, however, are needs that most of the time are not addressed and *definitely need to be taught, not only from a biblical perspective, but from a single adult perspective!* The single life, with its unique demands and problems, has specific challenges that require teaching and ministry with an understanding of the issues as they relate to singleness. For example, a person teaching on the topic of sexuality would need to present not only a different approach but different and additional information to single adults than to married adults. Biblical constraints regarding behavior for the single Christian are different and more restrictive than they are for the married Christian in the sexual arena.

Unfortunately, this and other specific single adult issues are rarely taught from this vantage point in the vast majority of evangelical and Pentecostal churches across our country. It seems that most pastors do not understand this, do not realize it, or do not prioritize it.

This sad realization leads to a question of profound consequence. If the church is not teaching on these issues from a biblical and single adult perspective, *from what sources are single adults getting their information?* The answer to this question is glaringly apparent. The sources that are feeding, modeling, and teaching single adults their morals and principles concerning these life issues include:

- the movie industry
- the television industry
- the video industry
- the magazine industry
- the Internet industry
- the newspaper industry
- friends (many are unbelievers)
- work associates (many are unbelievers)

Are these sources biblical and spiritually healthy? Are they modeling and teaching solid, biblically moral principles upon which to build a strong Christian life? The answer is an obvious, resounding *no!* It is time for the church to "step up to the plate." It is time for the church to realize and accept the responsibility of building strong single and single-again adults by intentionally teaching relevant, personal issues from both a biblical and single adult perspective. There are many Bible-teaching churches and groups in America that should be and could be consistently teaching these issues, and by doing so, they would be recognizing, reaching, restoring, and releasing single adults into the kingdom. It is imperative that they do so. The lives and futures of millions of single adults are at stake!

Basic Challenges the Church Should Help Meet

Accepting and Accommodating Singleness

It is true, sadly, that the world understands and accommodates the reality of singleness better than the church. I have seen and heard the truth of this statement from single adults who feel like a "fifth wheel" in many churches' marriage and family focused environments. Let me illustrate the point by contrasting some realities outside and inside the church.

Outside the church:

1. Grocery stores have sold food in servings for one for many years.
2. Restaurants plan table arrangements expecting to accommodate many who will be dining alone.
3. Businesses and companies hire responsible single adults for top management positions because they know a single adult can move to another city with less delay and without having to obtain agreement from a spouse.
4. Secular society does not question one's singleness as quickly or frequently as the church does. Singleness is accepted as a viable, normal lifestyle, and subtle or not-so-subtle pressure to marry is not as great in society as it is in the church.

Inside the church:

1. Churches set banquet tables for even numbers of people—six, eight, or ten—rather than set them for five, seven, or nine to anticipate single adults.
2. Pastors and key church leaders usually prefer married people over single people to fill important leadership roles such as the deacon board, elder board, and missions board.
3. Event registration and ticket costs for one are not always exactly half the price of the cost for two, creating a negative bias against single adults.
4. Valentine's Day banquets are designed and promoted with married and dating couples in mind. This is demonstrated by comments like, "Bring your sweetheart to the banquet," or, "Give your spouse a special night out." These remarks can cause single adults to feel alienated, alone, or not a part of the church family and do little to encourage them to participate.
5. Men's and women's retreats are commonly promoted in the same way. For example, announcements such as, "Ladies, talk to your husbands about attending the upcoming retreat," are too common. This automatically assumes every woman present is married when 30 to 50 percent of them are probably not.

These are just some of the examples of bias that is mostly unintentional but harmful nevertheless. Attitudes and comments like these tend to alienate single adults from full participation in the life of the church.

Assist in Building Quality Relationships with Males and Females

Single adults, whether never married or formerly married, have a God-given desire to establish and maintain quality relationships with members of both the same and the opposite sex. God's Word teaches that we are not created to be alone but are meant to enjoy and benefit from relationships with others (Gen. 2:18; Prov. 17:17; 27:6, 10; 1 Cor. 11:11). Married adults have the same need, but they have satisfied it, at least minimally, by being in a committed marital relationship (Eph. 5:22–31). The church could and should provide a healthy, safe, and effective place for single adults to meet, establish quality relationships, and even find godly mates in some cases.

The opportunity for single adults to discover and nurture relationships with members of the same and opposite sex has not been recognized or promoted, however, in the majority of churches in our country. Reasons for this were stated in chapter 2 in the section entitled, "The needs and issues of single adults motivate the need for this ministry." Because of this, many unmarried adults have looked elsewhere to satisfy this desire. *The world has capitalized* on the enormous numbers of single adults wanting to establish relationships by creating hundreds of meeting places, both Christian and non-Christian. One only needs to search (and not for long, either!) on the Internet under "singles," "dating," or one of many other key words to discover a diverse variety of opportunities to meet other single adults.

Other visible opportunities can be found by consulting the local newspaper, most magazines, or bulletin boards in shopping centers, etc., for advertisements. One could also visit bars and nightclubs all over the country boasting atmospheres and activities designed to connect singles looking for friendships or dating relationships. Unfortunately, these places have not always had the best environment or reputation and have led to "quick fix" relationships, unhealthy friendships, immoral attitudes and behaviors, or at best, short-term friendships and romantic relationships.

Seeing the spiritual, emotional, and relational carnage that exists in the lives of single adults, partially because of looking outside the church for quality relationships, one would think the church would understand and seize the opportunity and responsibility of providing healthy fellowship groups where single adults could meet. A specific ministry for single adults can provide an atmosphere of acceptance and openness where people can discover others with the same hopes, hurts, issues, and interests, and where they can establish relationships and friendships in a Christian context.

Lisa Stevko from Castro Valley, California, says, "I don't feel like I'm just waiting to be married anymore. The single adult ministry has provided me with a circle of friends and activities. I have others that I can talk and relate to that are being stretched and grown by God in the same ways I am."[2]

Certainly the desire of parents to see their young adults marry and the possibility of helping single and single-again people discover and nurture spiritually healthy relationships are good reasons to offer targeted ministries to help meet these particular needs. *If the church does not offer these opportunities, can we blame single adults for looking other places?* Would married adults realize this lack of opportunity for single adults to meet in a healthy atmosphere if they became single-again either by death of a spouse or death of a marriage? The answer is *yes*. It is ironic how needs caused by circumstances of chance, change, or choice (whether the person's or someone else's) can bring a new perspective and understanding. Many single-again adults and remarried adults have attested to this.

Affirming and Assisting Single-Parent Families

The single-parent family in the U.S. has reached approximately one third of all family types in the country.[3] There are currently 15 million single-parent families—almost all with difficult, stressful situations—who are attempting to meet the unique challenges of rearing children alone. Bobbie Reed offers four different types of attitudes single parents experience in responding to the demands of parenting alone.[4]

1. *"I can't do anything."*—These parents feel defeated, depressed, useless, and inept and appear immobilized until they can learn to just take things one step at a time.
2. *"I'll do it or die."*—These parents work themselves to death trying to do everything alone. They refuse to curtail any activity or chore and work at a fast pace, getting little sleep or relaxation. They need to be taught priorities of parenting and the need for and way to personal relaxation.

3. *"I'm surviving."*—These parents are hanging on by their fingernails, emotionally up one day and down the next. Their lives only begin to smooth out after they find their balance and confidence.
4. *"I'm doing my best."*—These parents are doing their best with the time, money, energy, and other resources they have. They realize all parents will make mistakes and there are no perfect parents.

How a Church Can Help

James 1:27 states, "Religion that God our Father accepts as pure and faultless is this: to look after orphans and widows in their distress." Single parents and their children are definitely some of today's widows and orphans! The local church is in a unique position to assist these families due to the love, compassion, and resources its people possess. Some of the needs of single-parent families and suggested ways of ministering to them include:

1. *Provide respite*—Many single parents do not have family close by and, consequently, have no time or little free time away from the children. They cannot afford child care for anything more than their work time, if even for this. The church could provide a monthly night out for single parents to attend an event, hang out with friends, or just be alone and read or watch a movie.
2. *Provide role models*—Single parents may desperately need a same-sex role model for a child to take him or her to events, talk about issues, go to the zoo, etc. Big brother and big sister programs are needed by these children. Christian men and women (both married and single) could provide a few hours per month to befriend and minister to these kids. Why should we let only the world try to meet these needs?
3. *Adopt a family*—Encourage church families of all types to adopt a single-parent family and include them in regular family

outings like picnics, trips to the zoo, or just getting together for dinner.

4. *Organize resources*—Single parents need help with common items that many people take for granted. They can benefit greatly from the provision of practical resources such as good used clothing, auto repairs, household repairs, occasional free child care, Christmas gifts, books for school, mending clothing, meals when the parent is ill, occasional help with utility bills, and discussion opportunities. Some ideas for providing these include:

- Organized clothing exchange day
- Oil change day—a quarterly day set aside to give free oil changes
- Light home repairs—a group of people willing and able to provide various home repairs throughout the year
- Quarterly offering in a church service to help with utility bills
- Christmas tree with cards hung on it giving the age and gender of needy children and parents for the congregation to take and provide gifts for
- "Recycled Christmas"—single parents bring the toys their children have gotten tired of or outgrown and exchange them for "new" toys someone else has brought
- Child care—free child care provided on a certain night of the month
- Support groups—weekly or biweekly groups for parents to discuss issues in their lives
- Occasional single-parent workshops on topics relevant to single parents with free child care provided

These are just a few of the ways a church should minister to its single parents. Invite single parents to a planning session to let them tell you what their needs are, then brainstorm ways the church could provide those needs. Remarried couples are often extremely understanding of single-parent needs, since many of them were single parents. They may also be willing to help provide creative solutions.

These three basic issues—accepting and accommodating single-ness, providing for the need for quality relationships with males and females, and affirming and assisting single parents—are only *three of the many challenges of singleness that a church could and should meet.* A church that ministers to single adults in these ways is certainly being sensitive to the needs of a huge percentage of society that is often relationally overlooked, emotionally undernourished, and spiritually starved.

Who Are Single Adults?

A Look at the Five Types

Objectives

1. Identify and describe the five types of single adults.
2. List the characteristics and values of young, never-married adults.
3. Show the positive acceptance usually displayed toward the widowed.
4. Show the lack of understanding and neglect churches usually display toward the divorced.
5. Acquaint the reader with the practical needs of single parents.
6. Offer observations concerning separated persons.
7. Offer an understanding of when and why a separated person may attend the single adult ministry.
8. Name basic needs common to most single adults that can be met in a single adult ministry.

Five Types of Single Adults

Almost anyone involved in ministry to single adults will readily accept the fact that there are at least four types of single adults—five if the separated person is included. These are:

1. The never-married person (always single)
2. The divorced person (single-again by death of a marriage)
3. The widowed person (single-again by death of a spouse)
4. The single-parent person (who may be single due to these or another of many reasons, which will be named in this chapter)
5. The separated person (single-again due to separation from his or her spouse)

The separated adult may or may not think of himself or herself as single and in some situations should be allowed to attend the single adult ministry. These situations will be addressed later in this chapter.

The Never-Married Person

"Dad, I like my life the way it is now. Besides, I'm not really ready to marry yet. There are too many things I want to do before I marry. What's the rush anyway?"

The single adult who is not yet married is usually a young adult in their twenties or early thirties but may be an adult in their forties or even older. Older unmarried adults are becoming more common. There are currently 48 million adults in the U.S. who have never married. The median age of marriage has increased significantly since 1970 to 27.1 for men and 25.4 for women.[1] Some are choosing to remain single longer to establish a career, finish a degree, purchase major life items, or pursue other goals. Some have not found their life's partner and are still waiting for this to happen.

Waiting to marry or not marrying at all in today's culture does not seem to carry the stigma it did thirty years ago. Society seems to accept singleness better than the church does, though. Thankfully, questions that used to be commonly vocalized in the church are not usually articulated and mostly remain as thoughts and questions in people's minds: "Aren't you a little too picky?" "Do you plan to remain single for the rest of your life?" "Why do you let all the good ones get away?" "Do you have something against marriage?" "When are you going to settle down?" "Are you gay?"

There are many important characteristics and traits of young adults in their twenties and thirties that influence a ministry targeted toward them. These include:

- importance of relationships
- individualism
- love of diversity
- self-sufficiency
- wary of institutions
- wary of commitment
- welcome change
- welcome risk
- spiritual seekers
- wary of boundaries
- embrace technology
- media savvy
- love of stories
- love of music

A church wanting to develop ministry to and with young adults needs to understand values that are important to young adults. They include:

- authenticity
- relevance
- ministry different than the past
- new music and styles of worship
- diversity, yet alignment with biblical values

- hands-on presentation of the gospel
- narrative stories to communicate
- leadership by team
- process evangelism
- lay leaders developing other leaders
- pastor's role as equipper

The Divorced Person

"You what?" Bill exclaimed emphatically.

"I want a divorce," Mary repeated.

"I can't believe it. We've been through rough times before and always worked things out," responded Bill.

A month later Mary moved out and filed for a divorce. Five months later, Mary and Bill were single again.

Divorced persons, suddenly single-again because of the death of a marriage, are usually hurting and find themselves in one of the stages of the grieving process (shock, anger, denial, depression, or bargaining) before they reach the acceptance stage. They need the church to be a safe place of acceptance and unconditional love for them to begin to heal. Unfortunately, it is not always so.

Christians sometimes tend to hurt the wounded with judgmental attitudes and comments. We may think we know the circumstances surrounding a divorce, but rarely, if ever, do we know enough of both sides to have an unbiased, intelligent opinion without discussing the problems with both parties. *It is so crucial to remain unbiased* and love both individuals as opportunities to do so present themselves. Widowed adults often feel the love and attention of the church the first month following a spouse's death through cards, letters, phone calls, meals, and visits. *Very rarely, however, does a divorced person receive this kind of love and caring!* Does this portray Jesus's command to unselfishly love each other as he has loved us?

There are currently twenty million divorced adults in the U.S.[2] The average length of a *first marriage is eight years;* the average length of a *second marriage is six years.*[3] In 1970 the divorce rate was 35 people out of 1000. In 1999, according to Christian researcher George Barna, the rate was 250 people out of 1000.[4] This represents a 680 percent increase! The bottom line: *one fourth of all adults* in the United States report having been through at least one divorce.

The attitudes and reactions of those facing divorce are diverse. Some are emotionally divorced long before the legal process begins and complete the mourning process before the separation. Some are shocked by the news of their partner desiring a divorce because they did not realize things were that bad. Some are relieved to be out of the relationship. Some find it very difficult to let their loved one go and struggle for months and years. Others do not want to let go of their married status and reject thinking of themselves as single now. Some remarry quickly to try to resolve their conflict with singleness.

Divorce brings many kinds of adjustments, fears, and relational, emotional, financial, and spiritual problems that deserve specialized ministry. Some churches have chosen to address these issues with divorce recovery workshops. Teaching and discussion on relevant issues the divorced person faces help to bring the necessary adjustment and balance to life again. Working with people going through a divorce can be very rewarding as they recover emotionally and spiritually. Adults who have fully recovered from divorce can be very effective in working with others going through the pain of separation and dissolution of marriage, whether it was their choice, their spouse's choice, or a mutual decision. Church leaders are wise to use them as "wounded healers" in the process of helping others recover.

The Widowed Person

"I am so sorry; we did everything we could to save her." The doctor's words cut his heart in two.

"Oh, God, what am I going to do?" John cried. He did not feel it yet, but he was suddenly a single adult.

Widowed people understand the phrase, "You may be only one heartbeat away from singleness." No one plans to become single through the death of a spouse. It happens all the time, though. Sometimes it is somewhat expected due to a long illness; sometimes it comes through a sudden, shocking accident.

There are 13.5 million widowed adults in the U.S., more than the entire population of each of the nations of Belgium, Ireland, and Norway. Of all women age sixty-five or older, 45 percent are widowed, and 70 percent of all widowed adults live alone.[5]

Widowed individuals do not feel single for a long time, some up to two or three years. After all, they did not choose this to happen and feel they are still married to their spouse; he or she is just not there. They experience many of the same problems, hurts, and grieving processes as a divorced person: they lose a spouse, lose the married status, must find and experience a different identity, must make decisions alone, and have to reestablish themselves in a society and church that is usually focused on marriage and family.

Churches that want to minister to the widowed adult need to persevere beyond the first month's cards, letters, phone calls, and visits. These are expected actions by the body of Christ, but the following months can be the most difficult as caring and love from others in the church subside.

Many widowed adults have had good marriages that have served as role models. These individuals can be valuable counselors, mentors, and support group leaders to others who are going through the process of adjustment after losing a spouse to death. They may more readily attend a ministry for single adults after two or more years have passed, or they may not ever become a part of this ministry because they feel it might be disloyal to their spouse. While at Bethel Church in San Jose, California, we began a weekly ministry class for widowed adults called "Living Again." This class continued for four years with teaching, discussion, and monthly activities. It obviously met real needs for many individuals.

The Single-Parent Person

"How am I supposed to raise my two girls alone?" Barry asked the pastor. "I don't know how; I was never a little girl."

There are over *twelve million* single-parent families headed by females and over *three million* single-parent families headed by males in the U.S.[6] These adults have become single parents through one of many causes:

- birthing a child while unmarried
- adopting a child while unmarried, divorced, or widowed
- acquiring a child through medical means (artificial insemination, in vitro fertilization, sperm bank)
- divorce
- widowhood
- separation
- foster parenting while unmarried
- raising someone else's child while unmarried

Twenty-four million children (nearly four out of ten) live in a home without a father. A full 60 percent of all children born in the 1990s will spend a significant amount of their childhood in a father-absent household.[7] Startling realities like these could fill several pages. Suffice it to say, our society has changed. Single parents are not the small minority they used to be.

I believe that being a single parent today is one of the toughest jobs on the planet. Sharing the host of challenging and pressing parenting tasks with another parent is difficult enough. Doing it alone would be an overwhelming task. Imagine having to cook, clean, wash, pay bills, give rides, attend school functions, help children dress, solve problems, help with homework, etc., by yourself without the help of another parent. No wonder many single parents are tired!

Some single parents have sole custody of their child(ren), some have joint custody, some have visitation rights only, and some have no contact with their children because of their own choice or the choice of the other parent. The custody situation alone is enormously stressful.

Single parents have a long list of practical needs, and they must have support and help from friends and the church if they are going to survive. Major needs of single parents include:

- acceptance
- understanding
- affirmation

- encouragement
- respite
- love
- vehicle repair assistance
- financial assistance
- time alone
- material assistance
- home repair assistance
- child care assistance
- time to be with adult friends

A church that ministers to single parents in practical as well as spiritual ways is a church that is fulfilling James 1:27, "The Christian who is pure and without fault, from God the Father's point of view, is the one who takes care of orphans and widows" (TLB). I believe that single parents and their children are many of the orphans and widows of today (see chapter 4 for additional ideas for ministering to single-parent families).

The Separated Person

It was stated earlier in this chapter that separated people should sometimes be allowed to attend a ministry designed for single adults. When separated individuals visit the single adult ministry, it will not always be easy to ascertain whether their marital status, or separation, is known to the group. Time and space do not permit a lengthy explanation concerning this, but the following observations about separated individuals may be helpful.

Although the separated person is legally married, he or she is *living the life of a single adult, especially if he or she has been separated for a long period of time.* The domestic tasks, financial responsibilities, child care duties, home repairs, car repairs, and all other responsibilities that were shared by the other spouse are now being done by one person. This person is, indeed, living as a single adult. It is usually only after a person feels there is little or no hope for reconciliation that a visit to the ministry will occur.

In most churches, the separated person usually has no place to turn for *consistent support*. He or she is hurting and may be embarrassed to let many know of his or her situation. Many times a separated person goes for weeks or months without proper support, understanding, and help from pastors, married adults, and others in the church. This person sometimes even leaves the church because of feeling no one understands or because of memories made at the church with a spouse. The exception to this situation is the married person who is involved in a class of married adults and has close friends within the group. This person should be pursued, loved, supported, and encouraged by the married class of which he or she is a part and with whom there are established bonds.

Usually (but not always) *when a separated person visits the single adult ministry, he or she has lost most or all hope of reconciling* with his or her spouse and will benefit from the acceptance, support, and learning from others in a single adult ministry. The experience others have gained from similar situations serves as a great teacher.

Extremely few churches have a targeted ministry toward separated persons or any training for the staff or congregation in personal, one-on-one ministry to them. This is probably due to the small number of separated people who actually make their separation known and the difficulty of continual, thorough ministry to them. These people have heavy issues and hurts, and most people in the church do not know what to say to them.

Although it takes two people to marry, it only takes one to divorce in today's society. Many individuals have become single due to their spouse divorcing them against their wishes. Although both parties usually share some percentage of the blame for the failure of the relationship, when one person decides to divorce, it is permanent more often than not. All states now have a no fault divorce law, which allows one spouse to divorce for no reason at all. "Not getting along" has become reason enough. It is legally termed "irreconcilable differences," or the marriage is "irretrievably broken." These individuals need somewhere to experience the healing and wholeness that unconditional love extended by God's people will bring.

Adults who are single-again due to a separation and divorce frequently help another separated person to see that the grass is not always greener on the other side. Divorce frequently creates as many problems as it solves. This is understood through relationships with other Christians whose yesterday is the separated person's today. It is also common for single adults to pray for reconciliation of someone's marriage.

It is much easier to identify a separated person in a small ministry than in a large one due to sheer numbers. However, there will be some individuals who will conceal the fact of their separation. So, when should a separated person be allowed to attend? There are no easy answers, and leaders working in single adult ministry will find there will be many opinions. Here are mine.

I would tend to allow a separated person to attend a ministry for single adults in the following circumstances and for one or more of these reasons:

1. When there seems to be no hope for reconciliation.
2. When you know the person has gone through a process of evaluation, reflection, prayer, and counseling over a long period of time and has come to the point of a genuine sense of God's release from the relationship.
3. When the person has repeatedly attempted counseling and reconciliation with the spouse to no avail.
4. When there is knowledge of the spouse becoming engaged to someone else. (Yes, sometimes a person will do this during a separation before a divorce is final.)
5. After careful consultation with and on the advice of close friends of the individual.

I would like to conclude with a few admonitions for working with separated adults:

Recognize that the Holy Spirit is active and will work with and guide the separated person who is committed to him. Too often people want to "police" the person who is separated and do not trust the Lord to guide and provide the information, inspiration, and direction needed.

It is very difficult to know both sides. Usually it is impossible! Even when a counselor has the opportunity of meeting with both parties of the marriage, one must recognize that many times the truth lies somewhere in the middle of the information given by both parties. Again, only God knows the complete picture, and we must trust him to work in the situation.

Resist the temptation to judge. It is very rare for any of us to know all the insights and answers to a marital separation. Leave the results to God.

Finally, there can be positive effects from allowing a separated person to attend a single adult ministry. I understand there are also potential dangers (dating, personal confusion, etc.). Yet I have also witnessed the positive effects of *unconditional love, acceptance, understanding, and guidance given to these people by individuals in the ministry.* I have seen the separated person gain an understanding that singleness has its own set of challenges and that divorce sometimes creates as many problems as it solves. Each person who is separated and visits the ministry should be treated on an individual basis. Again, this is easier to do in a small group. Large ministry groups may have to work diligently at discovering and working with the separated individual.

Basic Needs a Single Adult Ministry Can Meet

A healthy, balanced ministry will meet many basic needs that are common to all five types of single adults. If these basic needs are not met in and through the church, single adults will look elsewhere to fulfill them. Unfortunately, some of these places are spiritually, emotionally, and relationally unhealthy and contribute to further confusion and hurt. The needs that can and should be met through single adult ministry include, but are not limited to:

Achievement

Single adults need to experience a sense of achievement and contribution. A ministry to and *with* them affords opportunities for involvement in multifaceted ways and tasks. A person could be involved in ministry in something as simple as pouring coffee, distributing class materials, or setting up tables and chairs. He or she may also be spiritually mature enough to be a class teacher, discussion leader, prayer coordinator, or Bible study leader. There are many opportunities for single adults to acquire a sense of achievement through developing their talents and abilities in one of the many ministry tasks in single adult ministry.

Belonging

One of our deepest needs as humans is to belong, to feel included, accepted, and a part of something. The gospel message is all about belonging: belonging to Christ because of his sacrificial death for us, belonging to God the Father because of the purchase he initiated through his Son, and belonging to each other because of being a part of Christ's body. Single adults desperately desire and need to belong. Not having a spouse emphasizes this need and makes them prime candidates for becoming part of a group that will accept, love, and include them.

Companionship

The need for companionship is another basic need that can be met through a single adult ministry. God made us to need each other, males and females both needing relationship with both genders. One of the most beautiful Scriptures in the Bible is found in 1 Corinthians 11:11, "In God's plan men and women need each other" (TLB). This is not referring to the marriage relationship but to friendship and companionship. A group known as a safe place is one in which single adults can find and experience true, authentic friendship and companionship with males and females.

Hope

Jeremiah 29:11, another wonderful verse, expresses the hope that God has for each of us: "I know the plans I have for you, says the

Lord. They are plans for good and not for evil, to give you a future and a hope" (TLB). Single adults need to find hope for their life, hope for being accepted just as they are, hope for a bright future, and hope for becoming all God says they can become. A healthy ministry provides these through the teaching, fellowship, and healing that is experienced through God's love shown by his people.

Information

We live in an age of information saturation. The challenge is to obtain the right information necessary to live a godly, effective, healthy, and balanced life. Through single adult ministry, individuals have the opportunity to receive biblical and practical teaching and discussion opportunities on a variety of subjects that affect and interest them. As stated in chapter 4, if these topics are not addressed by the church, where are people going to receive their information? The answer is obvious: the world. Not only should a single adult ministry provide information regarding life issues and felt needs, but it should address spiritual issues such as salvation, prayer, commitment, discipline, obedience, baptism, etc.

Learning

There is a constant challenge to continue the learning process in life. One way we learn is through relationships with others, both males and females of the same approximate age and different ages. In an atmosphere of acceptance and safety, single adults learn a great deal emotionally, socially, relationally, financially, spiritually, and educationally from others.

Role Models

A ministry will have two basic types of people: *lifters* and *leaners* (see chapter 4). Lifters are individuals who are spiritually and relationally healthy and growing. They lift others up by their encouragement and example. Leaners are individuals who need to be lifted because of personal hurt, rejection, discouragement, etc.

Lifters can be role models for leaners. Their kindness and service to them as well as honesty, integrity, humility, and transparency serve as a role model for many others. Without being connected to a group such as this, many single adults have only unhealthy role models from which to learn.

Spiritual Growth

A person never outlives the need to grow spiritually. We have the opportunity of becoming more like Christ on this earth as we surrender to his purposes and ways in our lives. A single adult ministry will greatly assist in a person's spiritual journey and growth in many ways. Some of these include: Bible teaching, teaching of spiritual issues, teaching on personal issues/felt needs, discussion, observing and participating in prayer, and Christian fellowship. All growth is fostered and nurtured by the Holy Spirit through each of these as well as through direct, personal work that is accomplished in the heart and mind of each person as God wills.

Understanding

It is true that single adults can find acceptance through relationships in the whole body of the church. It is difficult, however, to find *experienced understanding* from individuals who have not gone through the same or similar circumstances. A single adult ministry affords many people with similar and same situations to offer genuine, experienced understanding.

An effective ministry to and with single adults will meet needs that cannot be met in a church that does not have this ministry. For confirmation of this, talk to a single adult who attends a single adult ministry in a church other than his or her home church. Reasons for attending the ministry will most likely include many of these listed as well as the fellowship, teaching, discussion, acceptance, or activities the single adult ministry offers.

Ministry Models

Discovering Which Is Right for You

Objectives

1. Acquaint the reader with basic elements that influence the structure of a ministry.
2. List several key questions that need to be discussed and answered before beginning one or several models of ministry.
3. List and describe several ministry models that should be considered.
4. Compare and contrast the benefits of hosting a ministry on or off the church grounds.

Ministry to single adults requires deliberate and strategic planning due to several variables that affect the target group and how a ministry is organized. One of these variables is *age*. Single adults cannot all be lumped into one category any more than married adults can be. A twenty-five-year-old married adult and a fifty-five-year-old married adult have little in common besides the fact that they are married. Lifestyles, issues, opinions, physical abilities, and perspectives are different due to their age and life experiences. So it is with adults who are single.

Another variable regards *single status*—the reason a person is single. As explained in chapter 5, single and single-again adults have different needs and issues based upon the reason they are single. A never-married person has not had to face the issues and resulting feelings that a person faces through a divorce. A divorced person has not had to face the feelings caused by the finality of a spouse's death in the way a widowed person has.

I am not, however, advocating ongoing segregation of the different types of single adults by single status without regularly meeting with the other types. Rather, I am advocating taking advantage of the ability to build a *targeted ministry to the special interest groups* for a period of time (e.g., single-parent families, divorce care, or widowed care) as well as encouraging them to attend an appropriate age group if this is offered in the same church. Usually it is only a large church that will have the ability to maintain several types of groups simultaneously.

Besides these two obvious factors, there are also *other variables* that affect the way ministry groups are planned and organized. Some of these include:

- purpose and mission of the ministry
- history and track record of any previous ministry
- philosophy of the senior pastor
- philosophy of the singles' pastor or leader
- philosophy of the leadership team
- demographics of the church
- demographics of the community
- consideration of similar ministries in nearby churches

These all influence the current and future structure and direction of a church's ministry to single adults and emphasize the diversity of people and the challenge of building a ministry designed to reach and teach them.

Answering Key Questions

There are several models of ministry to single adults today, each having its own purposes and characteristics. It is imperative for a church beginning or enhancing its ministry to evaluate several important questions that will help determine which model(s) of ministry is best. These questions should be discussed and answered by a team of people who are interested and going to be involved in the ministry. At the very least, the senior pastor, director of ministry to single adults, and a few other highly interested individuals should discuss and resolve these issues. By asking and answering these questions as a team, all will be involved in the process of owning and creating the ministry together. People will support what they help to create.

Examples of key questions to address include:

1. What is our mission statement (a definition of clear purpose)?
   a. Who are we trying to reach (Christians only, or non-Christians also)?
   b. What age group(s) are we trying to reach (nineteen to twenty-five, twenties and thirties, thirty-five and older, fifty and older, and so forth)?
   c. What need/special interest group(s) are we trying to reach (single-parent families, the divorced, the widowed)?
   d. Why are we trying to reach them?
2. What are the age and single adult demographics of our church? Take a survey or consult the church's database. A sample survey form can be found online at www.singles.ag.org under "Leaders/Training & Motivation." It is important to discover the types and ages of all single adults who call the church their home.
   a. never-married single adults
   b. divorced adults
   c. widowed adults
   d. single parents
3. What are the age and single adult demographics of our community? (All four types as in question two: never-married, divorced, widowed, single parents.) These demographics can usually be obtained from the county court house or online at the census bureau (www.census.gov).

4. What resources do we have now?
   a. potential leaders
   b. facilities
   c. materials
   d. other resources
5. What resources do we need to obtain?
6. Who else in our area is doing what we want to do?
   a. same church denomination
   b. other church denominations
   c. independent churches

Question six is important because not every church should feel it has to reach all single adults who live in the community. Small churches may not have the resources, budget, or leadership to target all types of single adults. Even large churches may elect to target only one or two of the age or need groups. For example, one church may excel in a divorce recovery ministry, while another church may excel in a single-parent family ministry. Since doctrine is not usually taught in a single adult ministry, church leaders should learn to feel comfortable referring someone to another church's ministry when their church does not provide for them. The bottom line is each church leader must determine direction regarding this issue.

Understanding Several Ministry Models

Let's examine several models of ministry being used today. As stated earlier, each of these has its own purposes and characteristics and emphasizes a particular type and style of ministry. Each model can be adapted to meet in the church building or off the church grounds in a home or other neutral setting. Each model will be described in three ways:

- Important elements
- Attracting and retaining people
- Minimum leadership recommended

The ministry models are:

1. Outreach
2. Discipleship
3. Discussion
4. Educational
5. Small Group
6. Social/Recreational
7. Contemporary Service
8. Combination

1. Outreach Model

This model is described first because of the appeal to both Christians and non-Christians and because it probably has the *greatest potential of all the models to attract the highest number of people.* Single adults like to see new people, and people attract more people. The more people attending, the greater the possibility of beginning other auxiliary ministries and models. Small churches should use a neutral location since they will not have enough single adults to grow an outreach model ministry within the church and people from other church backgrounds will not attend as easily if it is held in a small church.

In the outreach model, traditional Christian words and phrases are intentionally not used but are exchanged for terms that will relate to non-Christians and seekers. (*Programs* instead of *bulletins, guests* instead of *visitors, podium* instead of *pulpit, message* or *teaching* instead of *sermon, auditorium* or *room* instead of *sanctuary, audience* instead of *congregation,* etc.)

Important elements

Teaching—Time is dedicated to teaching personal issues/felt needs from a biblical perspective. Topics can include friendships with the same and opposite sex, self-esteem, identity, handling changes in life, sexuality, managing finances, dating, emotions, and so forth.

Seating—Informal seating using tables and chairs is best.

Discussion—Time should be set aside for discussion in almost every meeting, even if the teacher has to continue the lesson the next time. Discussion can be in the form of large group question and answer; small, guided groups; one-on-one, etc.

Fellowship—An extended time should be allowed (fifteen to thirty minutes depending on total time available).

Building/room—This model functions well in neutral, nonthreatening settings (rooms that are not formal and "churchy").

Praise and worship—Keep it light and short (two or three songs).

Prayer—Short prayers, usually by one or two people, can be included.

Refreshments—Providing refreshments can be very helpful for fellowship and helping newer people fit in.

Frequency of meeting—A weekly schedule works best to build momentum, especially if this is the only model being used.

Sponsoring church(es)—Any size church (small, medium, large) that has a passionate leader(s) can sponsor this model. Two or more evangelical churches of the same basic biblical beliefs can also jointly sponsor this model.

Tends to attract and retain

- mature and growing Christians
- nominal Christians
- non–Christians
- new Christians
- visitors
- people from all church backgrounds—especially if their church does not have a single adult ministry

Minimum leadership recommended

- outreach model coordinator
- teacher
- emcee
- music coordinator

- follow-up coordinator
- hospitality coordinator
- refreshments coordinator

2. Discipleship Model

The discipleship model is designed for Christians and functions well for the purpose of *helping them mature*. It does not normally attract and retain non-Christians well because of frequent use of the Bible, spiritual topics, and book studies and because most non-Christians do not understand, relate to, or comfortably know how to use the Bible.

Important elements

Teaching—Time is dedicated for teaching that focuses on Bible study and spiritual topics such as prayer, salvation, commitment, discipline, the Holy Spirit, the Trinity, baptism, and the second coming of Christ.

Seating—Informal or formal seating using tables and chairs is best.

Discussion—Time should be allowed for frequent discussion.

Fellowship—Social interaction can be encouraged, but it is not needed as much as in the outreach model.

Building/room—This model can function well in a church, home, or neutral setting.

Praise and worship—There can be an extended time for praise and worship, and it may be charismatic.

Prayer—An extended prayer time with many involved is appropriate for this model.

Refreshments—This is beneficial but not as necessary as in the outreach model.

Frequency of meeting—Weekly or biweekly meetings work best.

Sponsoring church(es)—Any size church can sponsor this model. Two or more churches of the same evangelical beliefs can also sponsor this model as long as the teaching is agreed upon and not doctrinally conflicting.

Ministry Models

Tends to attract and retain

- mature and growing Christians
- other church backgrounds—especially if their church does not have a single adult ministry
- does not attract and retain non-Christians and nominal Christians unless they are seeking
- does not attract as many visitors as the outreach model

Minimum leadership recommended

- discipleship model coordinator
- teacher
- music coordinator
- hospitality coordinator
- refreshments coordinator

3. Discussion Model

The discussion model is designed for both Christians and non-Christians. It attracts and retains both of them well since the topics discussed are not Bible topics that relate mostly to the spiritually mature Christian. Instead, the topics are personal issues/felt needs that single adults experience. Discussion is a major need of single adults since they go home to an empty apartment, a pet, or one or more children. They crave the benefit of adult conversation with both males and females.

Important elements

Teaching—Teaching is not the goal of this model. *Discussion is the goal.* Personal/felt-need topics such as friendship, self-esteem, identity, handling changes, dating, emotions, or managing finances are given a great amount of time to be discussed after a few relevant Scriptures are read and the topic is introduced by the group facilitator.

Seating—Informal seating is needed; tables and chairs or chairs in a circle are best.

Discussion—Except for the group moderator introducing the topic and key Scriptures, all the time (an hour) is dedicated to discussion in small groups (six to eight people) containing males and females.

Fellowship—Time should be set aside to encourage social interaction following the group discussion.

Building/room—This model can function well in a church, home, or neutral setting.

Praise and worship—A chorus or two (light and brief) may be included, but singing is not the goal.

Prayer—At the end of the discussion time each group can have a short prayer time. The "squeeze-hand method" works well. Group members hold hands, and the leader begins with a short prayer and then squeezes the hand of the person next to him or her. That person can either pray and then squeeze the hand of the next person or just squeeze the next person's hand if he or she is uncomfortable praying aloud or just chooses not to pray. The process continues around the circle until it gets back to the leader, who closes in prayer.

Refreshments—The fellowship time is benefited by providing refreshments.

Frequency of meeting—This can be weekly, biweekly, or monthly.

Sponsoring church(es)—Any size church can sponsor this model. Two or more churches of the same evangelical beliefs can also sponsor this model since the discussion centers around personal topics.

Tends to attract and retain

- mature and growing Christians
- nominal Christians
- other church backgrounds
- non-Christians—attracts them more easily in a nonthreatening, neutral setting
- visitors

Minimum leadership recommended

- discussion model coordinator
- one discussion leader/facilitator for each small group
- hospitality coordinator
- follow-up coordinator
- refreshments coordinator

4. Educational Model

The educational model is designed for educating and assisting single adults with either spiritual or personal/felt-need issues. It is held in a *seminar format* of three to eight evening sessions or a weekend format and functions well for churches that do not have the resources, leadership, finances, or vision to further develop a single adult ministry. It attracts and retains Christians and non-Christians, depending on the type of topics taught and discussed and the location of the meeting. Spiritual life topics will attract Christians more than non-Christians. Personal life topics will attract both.

Important elements

Teaching—Time is dedicated for teaching on either *spiritual topics* such as salvation, prayer, discipline, baptism, and the Holy Spirit, or *personal/felt-need topics* such as friendship, self-esteem, identity, handling changes, dating, emotions, and managing finances.

Seating—Informal seating is best using tables and chairs or chairs in a half circle.

Discussion—Discussion is needed after segments of teaching and can be done in small groups, large groups, one-on-one, or other types.

Fellowship—Time should be set aside before or following the teaching and discussion to encourage social interaction.

Building/room—This model can function well in a church or in a building off the church grounds.

Praise and worship—This should usually be light and brief.

Prayer—Light, short prayer times can be used to open or close sessions.

Refreshments—The fellowship time is benefited by providing refreshments.

Frequency of meeting—Scheduling two to four educational model times per year is appropriate for this model. Using "meetings" is confusing because one model session will meet three to eight weeks (or times).

Sponsoring church(es)—Any size church can sponsor this model. Two or more churches of the same evangelical beliefs can also sponsor this model if the teaching and discussion center around personal topics and the teaching is agreed upon and does not conflict with doctrinal beliefs.

Tends to attract and retain

- mature and growing Christians
- nominal Christians—especially if personal issues/felt needs are taught and discussed
- other church backgrounds
- non-Christians—especially if personal issues/felt needs are taught and discussed
- visitors—attracts them more easily in a nonthreatening, neutral setting

Minimum leadership recommended

- educational model coordinator
- discussion leaders/facilitators for each group
- refreshments coordinator
- music coordinator

5. Small Group Model

The small group model has at least two types: the *Bible study type* and the *prayer and share type*. The Bible study type is designed for and will attract and retain mature, new, and growing Christians.

The prayer and share type will also attract mature and growing Christians (especially if this is all that is offered) but is more designed for and will attract and retain nominal Christians and non-Christians. Mature, new, and growing Christians will soon want Bible study. As in the discipleship and outreach models, the study topics and discussions influence the type of individuals who will attend.

Important elements

- Teaching

  Bible study type—Time is dedicated to *teaching on spiritual growth topics* such as salvation, prayer, discipline, baptism, commitment, and the Holy Spirit.

  Prayer and share type—A limited amount of time is dedicated to teaching on personal/felt-need topics such as friendship, self-esteem, identity, handling changes, dating, emotions, and managing finances. Time given to teaching may not be as long as in the Bible study type, since the major components of the prayer and share model are *discussion, sharing, and prayer.*

- Seating—Informal seating is best with tables and chairs, sofas, or easy chairs.

- Discussion

  Bible study type—Discussion and sharing is needed after segments of teaching. Small group, large group, one-on-one, or other types of discussion groups are encouraged.

  Prayer and share type—Discussion and sharing are highly encouraged (as in the Bible study type); much more time should be allotted for discussion in this type of small group, though.

- Fellowship—Time should be allowed to encourage social interaction before or following the meeting.

- Building/room—Both types can function well in a church room, home, or other room in a building off the church grounds.

- Praise and worship

  Bible study type—Praise and worship may be intense, long, passionate, and charismatic.

  Prayer and share type—Time for praise and worship is usually shorter than in the Bible study type, and it is lighter and not as charismatic.

- Prayer

  Bible study type—Time for prayer may be extended, and prayers may be intense and passionate.

  Prayer and share type—Time for prayer may be extended, but prayers are short and light.

- Refreshments—This is beneficial for fellowship time, which usually follows the event.
- Frequency of meeting—Usually meetings are weekly or biweekly.
- Sponsoring church(es)—Any size church can sponsor both types of this model. Two or more churches of the same evangelical beliefs can also sponsor this model if the teaching and discussion is agreed upon and does not conflict with doctrinal beliefs.

Tends to attract and retain

- Bible study type

  Mature and growing Christians

  New Christians

  Other church backgrounds—especially if held in a neutral location

  Does not attract non-Christians easily

  Will attract Christians from other churches that do not have a Bible study for single adults

  Does not attract nominal Christians unless they are seeking

- Prayer and share type

  Mature and growing Christians

  New Christians

  Nominal Christians

  Non-Christians

  Visitors—especially if their church does not have a single adult ministry

  Other church backgrounds

Minimum leadership recommended

Both types basically need:

- teacher
- refreshments coordinator

- music coordinator
- host, if in a home
- discussion leaders/facilitators, if more than one group is used

6. Social/Recreational Model

The social/recreational model attracts both Christians and non-Christians and can be held in a church or at a *variety of social/recreational venues*. This model is used by churches that are in the beginning stages of developing a ministry to single adults or do not have the resources (leadership, facilities, finances, etc.) or vision to further develop a ministry to single adults. It is also used by churches that have other models in place and recognize that single adults want and need social/recreational activities. It does not provide structured teaching or discussion times since the activities are mainly for social interaction.

Important elements

Teaching—There is no formal teaching time.

Seating—This changes based on whatever the situation demands.

Discussion—Getting acquainted discussion and personal sharing take place as opportunities arise, but there is usually no structured discussion around a topic.

Fellowship—Social interaction is encouraged and is usually one of the highlights of the events.

Building/room—This model can function well in a church room, a room in a building off the church grounds, a home, a restaurant, or wherever the activity demands.

Praise and worship—Usually there is no praise and worship, although exceptions may be made before a meal or a banquet.

Prayer—No prayer time is planned unless a light, short prayer is included before a meal or to open or close a planned social or recreational session.

Refreshments—This is beneficial for fellowship time and to promote getting acquainted.

Frequency of meeting—As often as once a week or as little as a few times per year can work with this format. If this model is all that is offered, one or two activities per month will be needed to maintain interest.

Sponsoring church(es)—Any size church can sponsor this model. Two or more churches can also sponsor this model. If so, some church leaders may be concerned with doctrinal beliefs, but this really should not be a problem.

Tends to attract and retain

- mature and growing Christians
- nominal Christians
- non-Christians
- other church backgrounds—especially if their church does not have a single adult ministry
- visitors

Minimum leadership recommended

- social/recreational model coordinator or team
- refreshments coordinator
- follow-up coordinator

7. Contemporary Service Model

The contemporary service model seems to be used more today for young single adults (eighteen to thirty-five) than older single adults. It seems to attract and retain the younger better than the older due to the louder, contemporary music, extreme use of high-tech multimedia, drama, PowerPoint, low lighting, candles, etc. This model uses both spiritual and personal topics for teaching. It attracts and retains mature and growing Christians who want relevant teaching and fellowship and also nominal Christians and visitors fairly well because it tends to have a spectator, entertainment environment. The atmosphere can be described as fun, active, very casual, and yet spiritually and personally relevant. As in the outreach model, traditional words and phrases are intentionally exchanged for terms that will relate to non-Christians and seekers (*programs* instead of *bulletins*, *guests* instead of *visitors*, *podium* instead of *pulpit*, *message* or *teaching* instead of *sermon*, *auditorium* or *room* instead of *sanctuary*, *audience* instead of *congregation*, etc.).

Important elements

Teaching—There is a definite teaching time that is targeted to spiritual and relevant personal issues. The teacher is intentionally transparent, genuine, and knowledgeable and is a good communicator.

Seating—Informal seating is best and can range from chairs only to coffee tables, chairs, and sofas.

Discussion—Discussion usually is in the form of large group question and answer time. Intentional discussion groups are not usually the norm for this model, but they could be implemented if the room accommodates it and enough leaders are available.

Fellowship—Social interaction takes place before or after the event. Many groups have a coffee bar with coffee, tea, and snacks available for free or for purchase.

Building/room—This model can function well in a church room or chapel (the less churchy or traditional the better) or a room in a building off the church grounds. The room does not have to have elaborate decor or furnishings. Simple, warehouse-type rooms with relevant posters and decor are attractive to young adults.

Praise and worship—Usually there is a talented praise and worship band and leader. Time for praise and worship may range from fifteen to thirty minutes.

Prayer—Prayer may be at the beginning of the event, after worship, at the end of the event, or other times. Usually one person prays, unless there is a structured prayer/response time and others are needed to pray individually with people.

Refreshments—Providing refreshments is very helpful for fellowship time, further getting acquainted, and just hanging out together.

Frequency of meeting—This can be as often as once a week, bi-weekly, or monthly.

Sponsoring church(es)—Any size church can sponsor this model. Two or more churches can also sponsor this model. Some sponsoring church leaders may be concerned with doctrinal beliefs and would need to discuss their concerns.

Tends to attract and retain

- mature and growing Christians
- nominal Christians
- non-Christians—especially in a neutral location
- other church backgrounds—especially if their church does not have a young adult/single adult ministry
- visitors

Minimum leadership recommended

- contemporary service model coordinator
- refreshments coordinator
- hospitality coordinator
- follow-up coordinator
- music coordinator
- multimedia coordinator
- sound coordinator
- spiritual life coordinator
- drama coordinator

8. Combination Model

The goal of ministry to single adults is to meet as many of the diverse needs as possible with the resources available (staff, leadership, facilities, finances). Most churches will not be able to provide for all needs and issues, so the challenge is to decide which ministry models to begin. It is beneficial to begin several of the models, but not all at the same time. Generally, it is good to:

1. *Plan a total ministry.* This means that as God enables and resources are provided, many of the models will be used.
2. *Build the ministry in stages.* It takes time to plan, design, and construct the many parts of a building. The same is true of a ministry. It does not just fall into place but is carefully planned, prayed about, and implemented in stages.
3. *Wait until the vision is established.* The vision and purpose of a particular model must be clearly understood and articulated before the ministry begins.
4. *Wait until basic leadership is available.* It is foolish to begin a model before basic leadership is appointed and they understand the vision.
5. *Wait until resources are available.* It is premature to begin a model without the basic resources of facilities, finances, teaching materials, needed tables and chairs, etc.

Hosting the Ministry on or off Church Grounds

It is important to evaluate where the ministry should be held. A ministry event does not have to be held in a church building just because it is sponsored by one or more churches. I have intentionally held weekly, ongoing single adult ministry groups for years both on the church grounds and off the church grounds for specific reasons. The decision concerning where to host the ministry can and should be highly influenced by several factors:

- The size of the church(es) sponsoring the ministry—small churches do not usually attract large numbers of single adults inside the church building
- The model(s) chosen
- The advantages and disadvantages of hosting on or off the church grounds
- The size of the city

On the church grounds benefits

- more exposure of the people to the ministry of the host church

- more exposure of the ministry to the people of the host church
- fewer storage problems (coffee supplies, name tags, props, etc.)
- less set up, clean up, and transporting of tables, chairs, and materials
- more access to tables, chairs, props, etc.
- less time finding an appropriate meeting room
- usually less risk of losing the meeting room
- no cost for the meeting room
- fewer requests to announce other churches' events

Off the church grounds benefits

- more exposure of the ministry to the community
- attracts more non-Christians due to the neutral, nonthreatening setting
- attracts more Christians from other churches that do not have a single adult ministry at their church
- attracts more children of single parents (If the ministry is held on a Sunday morning during class time, children can be taken to the host church's classes and activities.)
- easier to build a citywide influence and image—especially in a smaller city
- easier to build relationships with other pastors. People from other churches will come, and a leader should be intentional about building relationships with these pastors.
- fewer denominational hang-ups in people's minds due to the neutral setting
- more flexibility of schedule
- any size church can sponsor the ministry
- easier for several churches to sponsor the ministry together

Elements to consider when hosting the ministry off the church grounds

- ample area for fellowship and seating
- flexibility of seating

- cost/rent of the room
- possible days room is unavailable
- image of the business from which you are renting
- location of the room
- storage of materials
- child care needs

Room ideas for off church grounds

- restaurant room
- hotel/motel ballroom
- community room
- apartment complex common room
- bowling alley meeting room
- bank meeting room
- service club room
- YMCA meeting room
- library meeting room

Designing Ministry for the Six Dimensions of Life

Objectives

1. Identify and emphasize the six dimensions of life: spiritual, social, mental, physical, relational, and emotional.
2. List and describe a variety of programs and activities that help meet various needs in these six dimensions of life.
3. List and describe advantages and disadvantages of designing ministry for the different dimensions of life.
4. Demonstrate that every church can minister to single adults by understanding some basic principles.

The Six Major Areas of Life

God created human beings to be multifaceted creatures comprised of at least six dimensions: spiritual, social, mental, physical, relational, and emotional. Each of these areas of life represents certain needs that can, in large measure, be met by the Lord and people in and through the ministries of the church. As stated in chapter 4, if these needs are not addressed by the church, single adults may look in other places for their fulfillment—places that are not always spiritually, emotionally, and relationally healthy. The six dimensions of life are:

1. *Spiritual*—helping a person develop his or her spirit and relationship with God.
2. *Social*—helping a person grow socially and *establish healthy relationships with groups of people*, both males and females.
3. *Mental*—helping a person continue learning in a variety of areas that will affect and increase his or her knowledge, wisdom, and understanding.
4. *Physical*—helping a person develop physical skills and maintain relatively good physical fitness.
5. *Relational*—helping a person *establish healthy relationships* with individuals of the same and opposite sex.
6. *Emotional*—helping a person understand and manage his or her emotions.

Each of these six areas can be targeted and developed in the lives of single adults by planning ministries that address the specific needs to be met and skills to be learned in each area. This chapter will identify numerous programs and activities that relate to each life dimension.

The programs and activities in a multifaceted, aggressive single adult ministry may need to be more varied and diverse than those in a youth, women's, men's, or seniors' ministry because of two distinct reasons:

1. The vast age range of single adults who will potentially attend (nineteen to sixty-five years old)
2. The five types of single adults who will potentially attend, each with unique as well as similar needs (never married, divorced, widowed, single parent, separated)

Most leaders design ministries around age groups because of similar life circumstances and needs. For example, middle school teens have different needs and circumstances than high school teens, so teaching and activities may be different for the two groups. It is the same principle with single adults. A twenty-five-year-old male has different needs, interests, and life issues than a forty-five-year-old male. These men may desire and need different opportunities to meet their needs and discover and develop their skills.

The additional factor, however, that makes single adult ministry even more challenging is the *diverse types* of single adults. The five distinct types listed in number two above each have similarities, but they also have many differences, which create the need for targeted programming and ministry opportunities (see chapter 4). These diverse needs should be kept in mind when planning ministry that falls into the six dimensions of life. Let's consider some of the more important needs that can be met and skills that can be taught in each of these six areas of life.

Spiritual Life

Examples of events that usually foster spiritual growth include but are not limited to: retreats, discussion groups, Bible studies, prayer meetings, community service or outreach projects, support groups for addictions, Sunday school classes, divorce recovery groups, conferences, seminars and workshops, mentoring programs, and prayer and share groups. Events such as these include teaching and discussion and are conducive to helping a person grow spiritually.

Teaching topics that foster spiritual growth include but are not limited to: salvation; discipleship; forgiveness; prayer; water baptism; commitment; Holy Spirit baptism; Bible teaching; obedience; compassion; fellowship; repentance; discovering, developing, and using spiritual gifts; commitment; dedication; trust; faith; grace; sanctification; holiness; righteousness; and relating to unbelievers.

Social Life

Examples of social life skills include but are not limited to: fun, laughter, experiencing new activities, developing existing social skills, learning new social skills, and learning to feel comfortable around the opposite sex. *Examples of activities* that are conducive to a growing social life include but are not limited to: parties, dinners, game nights, picnics, banquets, snack times, attending sporting events (ball games, rodeos, stock car races, etc.), barbecues, and visiting local attractions, festivals, or zoos.

Mental Life

Examples of mental growth skills include but are not limited to: stimulating the desire to learn, discovering and learning about new careers, developing mental concentration, using and developing the imagination, discovering new areas of interest, and growing educationally and intellectually. Seminars, workshops, and classes should be taught on a variety of subjects from a biblical and single adult perspective. Topics chosen should be conducive to helping a person grow mentally. *Topics of teaching and discussion* include but are not limited to: finances, self-esteem, dating, friendships, sexuality, identity, career planning, setting goals, attitude, memory improvement, and various educational and career topics.

Physical Life

Examples of growth in one's physical life include but are not limited to: staying physically fit, increasing strength, losing weight, learning new physical skills, improving existing skills, and having fun. *Activities that foster good physical fitness* include but are not limited to: bowling, roller skating, ice skating, softball, volleyball, water skiing, football, soccer, basketball, hockey, swimming, exercise classes, walking, hiking, rock climbing, running, bicycling, weight loss classes, physical fitness classes, tennis, golf, and badminton.

Relational Life

Examples of activities that promote a healthy relational life include but are not limited to: parties, discussion groups, book clubs, hobby clubs, dinners, sporting events, coffee houses, social activities, and recreational activities. *Topical teaching and discussion* on developing healthy relationships could include but are not limited to topics such as: developing healthy friendships, dating/courting, understanding the opposite sex, managing anger, accepting and receiving forgiveness, single parenting, stepparenting, loneliness, rejection, relating to married adults, becoming a marriageable person, premarital education, re-marital education, gossip, selfishness, and accepting singleness. These issues should be taught and discussed from a biblical and single adult perspective in a single adult ministry.

Emotional Life

There are many *emotional growth goals* for single adults that should be a part of single adult ministry. These include but are not limited to learning to understand and control emotions, experiencing fun and joy, learning to accept and give forgiveness, improving emotional stability, learning from the opposite sex, affirming the same and opposite sex, improving self-esteem, and growing in humility, honesty, integrity, transparency, kindness, and courtesy.

Examples of events or activities that help a person grow emotionally include but are not limited to: support groups (alcohol, nicotine, single parent, food addictions, weight loss, etc.), discussion groups, prayer groups, reading groups, professional counseling, and listening to and learning from others who have had similar experiences. *Teaching topics* that are conducive to emotional growth include but are not limited to: understanding and managing emotions, divorce recovery, many facets of widowhood, understanding grief, acceptance, bitterness, understanding my emotions, accepting singleness, depression, guilt, hope, jealousy, and stress.

Choose Direction and Develop Ministries Carefully

In chapter 6, "Ministry Models: Discovering Which Is Right for You," leaders are challenged to decide which model or models of ministry fit their philosophy, circumstances, and unique characteristics of their church before designing a ministry for single adults. The same principle applies when understanding and addressing the various dimensions of life and meeting the needs each area represents. Deliberate and purposeful planning should be used to achieve intentional goals and meet the specific needs of each dimension. Single adults are whole people comprised of at least these six dimensions (as are married adults). A church is wise to consider meeting as many of these life dimensions as possible when ministering to and with single adults.

There are certain advantages and disadvantages of designing ministry for any one or more of these dimensions of life. In her book *Single Adult Ministry for Today*, Bobbie Reed proposes four approaches churches use in meeting the six dimensions of a person's life: no ministry, a social program, a spiritual ministry, or a balanced ministry.[1]

No Ministry

A church may decide not to pursue a targeted ministry to single adults. This means there would be no Bible studies designed for them, no seminars or workshops, no discussion groups, and no social or recreational activities specifically geared to single adults. In essence, all single adults would be expected to be attracted to and attend any adult classes and functions, regardless of the audience they were intended to attract and minister to. Even though some of the classes would be designed for specific groups (such as married adults, senior adults, or college adults), single adults of all ages would be expected to have their needs and issues met in these classes. There would be no events specifically targeting single adults. Their unique needs would not be addressed.

For a little while, this approach would seem to have no negative consequences. After a short time, however, adverse realities would begin to reveal themselves. The following list speaks for itself.

Disadvantages of having no ministry for single adults

- The single adults who do continue to attend are led to believe (by omission and implication) that their needs are not as important as those of married adults.

- Some single adults will continue to attend basic services in the church (mostly Sunday morning) for their spiritual needs but will seek to have their social, mental, physical, emotional, and relational needs met outside the church. This can be very unhealthy depending on where they look.
- Some single adults will look for and attend another church that does address and provide for the unique needs and issues of single adults.
- Some single adults will drop out of the church completely, disillusioned and disappointed that Christian leaders (many of whom are married and are seemingly ignorant of single adults' needs) do not seem to care for them.

One haunting question deserves to be asked at this point. Would this approach be used in most churches for youth, children, or families? I think the answer to this is very obviously *no!* There really are *no advantages* to this approach of ministry to single adults.

A Social Program

Some churches do not separate or target single adults for spiritual teaching and ministry but do acknowledge that they have unique social needs. The social activity leaders plan functions under the name and umbrella of the particular church. These leaders of the social activities are usually from the church, but there may be little or no investment from the church pastors or elders, who are busy with the children's, youth, men's, women's, family, seniors', or other ministries deemed to have a higher priority. The social activity leaders may or may not be appointed by church leaders and may be left to fend for themselves much of the time. This scenario portrays the attitude that "as long as the single adults have some social events to help them find friends, they will be alright."

When the emphasis is only social and not spiritual also, single adults tend to identify with the group and with each other more than with the church itself. "The church lends its name, sanction and facilities and provides nominal supervision and promotion. The program will continue as long as the single adults remain actively involved, but it may be discontinued if interest wanes or the facilities are needed for a higher priority program."[2]

Advantages of having at least a social program

- This ministry requires little investment from the church in terms of time, energy, money, and commitment.
- It provides a simple way to have a single adult program.
- It keeps some single adults from going to another church in search of a single adult ministry.
- It may sometimes help draw in some single adults who would not ordinarily come to a church.
- This allows the church to start slowly and check the possible responses to a more developed single adult ministry.
- Single adults are encouraged to interact with and learn from each other.

Disadvantages of having a social program only

- It is only a program and not much of a ministry.
- There will usually be a lack of spiritual emphasis.
- It will not meet the spiritual, mental, and educational needs of single adults.
- It may not meet the physical and emotional needs of single adults.
- There may be a mistaken belief that the needs of single adults are being met because there is a *program* for them.
- The single adult program may be isolated from the total church program.
- The single adults may not be integrated very effectively or involved very extensively in the total life of the church.

A Spiritual Ministry

Another option is to design a ministry that focuses only on the spiritual needs of single adults. There is little concern for identifying or dealing with their mental, social, relational, physical, or emotional needs. The ministry is designed to evangelize and teach single adults concerning the spiritual issues in their lives.

There may be Sunday classes, weekday Bible studies, discussion groups, outreaches to the community, or other spiritual ministry opportunities. However, the focus of the teaching and discussion is mainly on spiritual issues (as in other adult classes the church offers), and the unique issues of single adults are not actually addressed. Single adults are given a class *because they are considered different from married adults*, not necessarily because they have different needs.

This approach shows that church leaders really do not understand the challenges of living as a single adult. Social events and other activities designed for fellowship and personal and relational growth are rare. Consequently, single adults tend to identify with the church rather than with other single adults.[3]

Advantages of a spiritual ministry only

- This ministry requires only a minimum investment from the church in terms of time, energy, or money.
- It provides a fairly simple way to have a ministry with single adults.
- It keeps many of the single adults attending the church.
- Single adults are encouraged to get together and enjoy and learn from one another.
- It emphasizes spiritual things such as Christian growth and reaching others for Christ.
- It provides a solid spiritual foundation for single adults who participate, and it can lead to a strong core group of those who faithfully attend.

Disadvantages of having a spiritual ministry only

- It attracts mainly the conservative and sincere seeker of God's Word.
- Many weak Christians and non-Christians are not attracted and retained.

- It minimizes or ignores the very real needs and problems faced by single adults in their daily lives.
- It isolates the spiritual side of people rather than assisting them in integrating a biblical perspective into all aspects of life. (There are many issues unique to single adults that deserve to be addressed by the church.)
- The entire realm of practical theology that integrates the total life experience, the church community experience, and the biblical perspective is ignored.
- It discourages openness and honesty about one's personal failures that are seen as a direct result of lack of trust in God.
- It tends to exclude the non-Christian who is looking for spiritual help but is not yet ready to embrace Christ as Savior and Lord.

A Balanced Ministry

The balanced approach to ministry is best because it ministers to the *whole person in all dimensions of life*. It recognizes that single adults are a unique group of people who share special challenges and face similar life decisions. Bobbie Reed so aptly states: "Single adults have some basic needs that are identifiably different from those shared by adults in general and married couples in particular. A balanced ministry is designed to meet these specific needs. Opportunities are provided for personal as well as spiritual growth, for relational as well as individual development, in an atmosphere of openness, honesty, Christian love and acceptance."[4]

With the balanced ministry approach, single adults will identify with both the church and the single adult ministry. It is also the most consistent approach, providing scriptural principles about relationships within the family of God as well as the function and purpose of the church. It takes seriously the instructions in God's Word for taking care of the widows, orphans, strangers, and the poor (Exod. 22:21; 23:9; Lev. 19:33; Deut. 24:14; Job 31:16–23; James 1:27).

Bobbie Reed's insightful comments concerning these people groups deserve repeating at this juncture:

Ministries with single adults and their families focus in unique ways on *widows, formerly married men and women, never-married adults, orphans* (children who have lost one or both parents or whose parents no longer live together), *strangers* (men and women who have no families to care for them), *the poor* (single adults who are struggling to make ends meet, especially single parents with custody of minor children), and *the oppressed* (single adults who are not being accepted by the church at large because of their divorce or their illegitimate children).[5]

The apostle Paul says that not caring for our own in very practical ways demonstrates that we have not understood the true meaning of Christian faith and community (1 Tim. 5:8). With this strong admonition from one of the greatest apostles from whom we continually preach, teach, and learn, how can a loving, caring church *not* care for these single individuals and their families?

In this balanced approach to ministry to single adults, the pastors and other *church leaders must take time to get to know and understand* many of the single adults and their issues and needs. The single adult ministry becomes a part of the total ministry of the church and will eventually need and deserve budgetary commitment, as most ministries of the church receive.

In summary, the balanced approach to ministry to and with single adults is the most effective, complete, and biblical approach and should be planned and implemented carefully, as in any other ministry of the church (youth, children, music, seniors, etc.). A multifaceted, balanced ministry should be planned when possible, even though it may take months or years to fully develop.[6]

Advantages of a balanced ministry

- A balanced ministry provides a mechanism for meeting the needs of the total single adult within the church structure.
- It can be designed to attract single adults of all ages and types (single by chance, single by choice, widowed, divorced, single parent).
- It keeps a strong spiritual emphasis while encouraging personal growth.

- Single adults are reached for Christ without driving away those who are not yet ready to adopt the Christian lifestyle.
- It provides a way for single adults to interact, not only together but also with the entire church family.
- It encourages honest, open expressions of personal growth as well as personal failure in the struggles of daily living.
- Christian love and acceptance is expressed for people who often wonder if anyone, even God, actually cares.

Disadvantages of the balanced approach to ministry

- It requires a great deal of planning, organization, and administration.
- It requires a high level of commitment.
- It requires an investment of time and other resources.

Any Church Can Minister to Single Adults

I believe that any church, no matter what the size, can be aware of, accept, and address some of the needs of single adults. *At the very least, a church of any size without a ministry to single adults can*:

- Acknowledge single adults through the teaching and preaching by including them in the messages and lessons. For example, "Whether you are married or single, there is a place for you in our church." And, "Jesus lived an effective life of ministry as a single adult."
- Give examples of effective single adults in Scripture such as Jesus, Paul, John the Baptist, Mary, Martha, Anna, the Samaritan woman, Timothy, Titus, Mary Magdalene, Deborah, Hagar, Dinah, Miriam, Naomi, Vashti, and others (see chapter 1 for more information).
- Provide respite, encouragement, support, and material and financial assistance for single parents, their children, and the widowed (see chapter 4 for ideas).

- Be aware of *other churches* in the community that *do have* a ministry for single adults and encourage your single adults to attend one of these groups for their emotional, mental, relational, physical, and social needs. Many single adults would welcome a pastor's recommendation of a church with a ministry specifically for them, and most would return to their home church to meet their spiritual needs.

When evaluating which approach to ministry your church might take, strongly consider utilizing the balanced approach. A total ministry could be planned initially but be built slowly in stages. Or a church might regularly have only one type of event to meet each of the six dimensions of life; for example, one Bible study a week, one social activity a month, one seminar every three months, one community outreach every six months, and one retreat a year. In this way a church would at least be minimally meeting some of the diverse needs of single adults.

Primary Characteristics of a Single Adult Ministry

Objectives

1. List and describe the basic characteristics of a ministry to single adults.
2. Explain biased labels people sometimes use to describe the ministry and some of the single adults who attend it.
3. Identify the primary need of single adults as quality friendships and relationships with males and females.
4. Identify and describe four major realizations from which a church with a single adult ministry will learn and benefit.

Who Will Attend?

As explained in chapter 4, there are five types of single adults who will be attracted to and attend a ministry labeled single adult ministry. Most of these could be almost any age, however for purposes of clarity and understanding, I will give an average age range of those likely to attend for each type.

Never-married adults—Most in this category are between eighteen and thirty-five years of age, but the majority who attend will be over twenty-nine because adults younger than that do not consider themselves to be "single." They don't identify themselves by their marital status, and to them, singleness describes someone older, usually in their late thirties and older. These individuals would feel more comfortable in and would be more likely to attend a group known as a "college age ministry" (ages eighteen to twenty-five) or a "young adult ministry" (midtwenties to thirty-five years old).

Divorced adults—Divorced individuals between thirty and sixty-five years of age will most likely attend a single adult ministry.

Widowed adults—Widowed adults between thirty and sixty-five years of age will most likely attend a single adult ministry. (There are older adults who are widowed, but they do not tend to identify with a single adult ministry).

Single parents—Single parents between twenty and fifty years of age will most likely attend also.

Separated adults—Some of these adults between twenty-five and sixty-five years of age will attend this ministry. (This person is legally married but is living a single lifestyle.)

Potential Labels—The Five *L*'s

There are many common myths, misunderstandings, and biases about some single and single-again people today, many of which were identified in chapter 3. Because of these biases, people sometimes give labels pertaining to single adult ministry and some of the people who attend. These labels can be summarized into five categories that I refer to as the five *L*'s (see table 8). The first four express a negative connotation and seem to be verbalized more in the church than in society.

Table 8 The Five *L*'s

The ministry/group	The people
Lonely hearts club	Loners
Dating market	Lovers
Hospital	Losers
Church	Leavers
Place of/for ministry	Livers

These labels express what some individuals perceive a ministry to single adults to be. When this bias is verbalized, it tends to discourage some people from visiting a ministry group. I would be the first to admit it is true there are lonely people who attend groups for single adults; it is true there are people looking for dates in a ministry group for single adults; it is true there are hurting people who attend single adult ministry groups. It is also true there are individuals who consider their single adult ministry group to be their church and do not involve themselves in any other area of the church, including the Sunday service.

It is important to point out, however, that *it does not take being single to be lonely!* The loneliest person in your town tonight is not a single adult but a married adult who is in a horrible marriage. This person is wondering, "Lord, can it get any worse than this?" This married adult knows what loneliness is.

A person does not need to be single to be hurting. Many married adults are hurting from the pain of rejection, misunderstanding, lack of affection, verbal and physical abuse, pornography, adultery, and many problems that can be part, although sometimes a hidden part, of a Christian marriage.

It is also true that some single adults are looking for a date or mate in a single adult ministry. As was stated earlier, however, I would rather a man or woman look for a date or mate in a Christian group, where the chance of relating to Christian men and women with biblical morals and values is much higher than places the world offers!

Considering the labels *hospital* and *losers*, it needs to be understood that we are *all* losers without Jesus Christ as our Savior and Lord. Singleness certainly does not necessitate the word *loser*.

People who use the labels *loners, lovers, losers,* or *leavers* concerning single adults or use the labels *lonely hearts club, dating market, hospital,* or *church* do so out of fear, insecurity, ignorance, pride, and disrespect. In reality, all of us, Christian or non-Christian, have areas in our lives that are weak and are not Christlike. The same exact labels could be used for some of the people in almost any church today.

Healing and Wholeness

The last label, *a place of/for ministry,* and the word *livers* used to describe people who are growing and serving in some capacity is the correct, healthy perception of a single adult ministry. This is, in reality, the goal of a ministry to single adults: to help an individual become the whole person God intended him or her to be spiritually, relationally, emotionally, socially, physically, and mentally.

Some individuals will come into the ministry hurting for one or more of many reasons: divorce, the death of a spouse, the breakup of a dating relationship, the loss of a job, the death of a loved one, problems raising children as a single parent, problems with alcohol or drugs, guilt from a behavior they know is wrong, and so forth. These people need the message of love, forgiveness, and healing Christ can give to them as well as the comfort and encouragement that Christian fellowship can bring to their lives. Through God's love, salvation, and direction they will grow. Through the Word of God they will grow. Through the teaching and discussions they will grow. A single adult ministry is characterized by healing and wholeness.

Emergency Room

Sometimes this road to healing and wholeness will require some emergency assistance. One should not be in leadership in a single adult ministry if he or she is not willing to accept a midnight phone call with a plea for help. These will come from people who are desperately hurting because of one of the issues mentioned above. Sometimes people need help right now! The leader needs to antici-pate "emergency room" type phone calls and other encounters that are a cry for help and direction. It is important to be sensitive to these interruptions and see them as opportunities for one-on-one ministry along the road to healing.

Common Issues and Needs of Single Adults of All Ages

Many of the needs and issues in the lives of single adults were listed in chapters 4 and 5. It is this author's belief that single adults deserve biblical teaching and discussion opportunities on these and other issues that are relevant to their lives. The following list identifies many of the *personal* needs and issues that single adults, regardless of age and type, will usually *have in common*. These are in addition to the *spiritual* issues of salvation, commitment, discipline, prayer, the Holy Spirit, water baptism, spiritual growth, etc.

- friendships with the same sex
- friendships with the opposite sex
- money management
- managing sexuality
- managing stress
- managing change
- learning to risk
- identity
- premarital education
- re-marital education
- managing emotions
- loneliness
- dating/dating again
- self-esteem
- setting goals
- dealing with guilt

In addition to the needs common to all single adults, there are many personal issues and needs they may face due to their particular age or life circumstances:

- rearing children alone
- shared parenting
- relating to a former spouse
- time away from children
- giving and receiving forgiveness
- learning to trust again
- divorce recovery
- finding my new role
- grief recovery
- learning to risk
- depression
- managing anger
- blending families

Healthy Friendships

The desire and need for quality friendships with people of the same and opposite sex is probably one of the biggest needs of single adults. Healthy friendships and compatible relationships are desired probably more by single adults than married adults. Married couples go home to a spouse who is, hopefully, also a friend. They share their life's hurts, hopes, desires, surprises, dreams, almost everything together.

Most single adults do not have a friend to go home to and share all of these things. Many go home to an empty apartment with four walls, a dog or cat, or a child. The church should be one of the main places where there are opportunities for quality friendships to form. If the church does not provide these opportunities, single adults will look elsewhere—many times turning to unhealthy places the world offers.

Developing healthy friendships with males and females is certainly one of the goals of a single adult ministry, and it is a desire of many of the people attending. Leaders need to be aware of the relationship dynamics taking place in their groups for personal and ministry reasons. As Bill Flanagan states, "We need to capture the special opportunity that is ours to provide a seedbed for developing relationships, while at the same time speaking to the spiritual vacuum and human needs of the single adults we influence."[1] A ministry to single adults is really a "meet market" where people can meet and develop authentic relationships in a nurturing, caring, wholesome atmosphere. The other type of "meat market" should be vocally discouraged and disapproved of to assure that the beauty and reality of Christian love and acceptance will be displayed.

Openness and Honesty

Single adults want to be told the truth about life and its hurts, complexities, and issues. There is no reason to beat around the bush with them. Issues such as sexuality, relationships, handling emotions, managing money, and other relevant topics need to be taught in a bold, frank, open, yet genuine way. They want to be told how it really is and will respect a teacher's honesty and candidness. Even when one may think the truth will offend them, it is better to be honest and forthright.

They also need to know the reason for the truth, however. For example, it is incomplete and somewhat misleading to only hear that sex outside of marriage is wrong and against God's will. Christians already know this, and they deserve to be given reasons that will provide greater understanding for God's commands.

Non-Christians also need to know reasons other than "God says so" that will make sense to them. Single adults, who live in a world where premarital sex is readily accepted, need and deserve to know the psychological, emotional, physical, and spiritual reasons why God asks us to wait for sex until we are in a lifetime, legal commitment. This is the type of honest, bold, candid teaching that will help a person have the tools to say *no* to sex outside of marriage.

Types of Counseling

Counseling individuals will be an ongoing task for a leader in a ministry to single adults. There are basically four types of issues that will dictate counseling needs.

1. *Spiritual issues* such as God, Jesus, the Holy Spirit, salvation, prayer, discipline, obedience, water baptism, finding God's will, and knowing right from wrong in the gray areas.
2. *Relational issues* such as friendships, dating relationships, forgiveness, jealousy, divorce, or parenting.
3. *Emotional issues* such as self-esteem, anger, impatience, bitterness, grief, widowhood, or the death of a family member or friend.
4. *Psychological issues* such as addictions, codependency, extreme low self-esteem, or mental illness.

The single adult ministry leader does not have to feel totally qualified to handle all types of counseling needed. The larger the group, the greater the need will be and the less one will be able to fulfill all counseling needs. The wise leader will establish relationships with Christian counseling offices in the area and refer individuals to them.

Mobility and Transience

One of the difficult realities of this ministry is the turnover of people. Single adults will come in and out of the ministry perhaps faster than in any other ministry in the church. Until they are grounded spiritually and are part of a small accountability group or have some other means of accountability, there is no one for them to be accountable to as married couples have with their spouse. Leaders may ask themselves, "What am I doing wrong that so many people come and go like water through a sieve? Why can't we retain more of our visitors?"

There are many reasons single adults leave a group. Some of them include:

- a move
- unfriendliness of some in the group
- conviction
- breakup of a relationship

- other involvement in the church
- too much spiritual emphasis
- too little spiritual emphasis
- stereotyping people
- no one in the group interests them
- marriage
- they are offended
- few in the group their age
- philosophical differences
- not comfortable with singleness

The back door can only be closed so far. People will come and go if, when, why, and where they want to. Don't worry about it. Love them while they are there, whether it is one time or a hundred times.

Entrances and Exits

Someone said there are three types of doors in a single adult ministry. These three doors need to be present to minister to the diverse types of people who will come in and out of this ministry.

Open Door—Everyone is accepted regardless of social status, race, religion, gender, or mental, physical, or social handicap.

Revolving Door—Everyone will leave the ministry—some immediately, some later, all eventually.

Sliding Door—Many single adults will become involved in another area of the church: greeters, choir, ushers, teachers, men's ministry, women's ministry, seniors' ministry, various boards and committees, etc. This is a good thing. Another goal of ministry to single adults is to help them become involved in the total life of the church, rubbing shoulders with married adults, senior adults, men, women, children, and youth. The church will become educated concerning the needs and issues of single adults as they become comfortable in the total life of the church and take positions of leadership.

Visitors

Because of the realities of the revolving door and sliding door and the mobility and transience of single adults, a ministry to single adults will constantly need to have new people coming into the group(s). If there are no new people visiting the ministry, it will eventually die. Visitors will be attracted by various means: personal invitations from friends, church promotion, individual curiosity, personal hurt or pain, and so forth. A general rule is that 10 percent of the total attendance of a group should be new people to maintain the current number of individuals. If a group has a lower percentage, it may begin losing numbers. If a higher percentage are visitors, it will usually grow in numbers.

When a continual lack of new people is noticed, the leadership team should evaluate the possible reasons why and make appropriate changes. Issues that should be evaluated include:

- mission and purpose
- promotion
- friendliness of the group to new people
- format of the meeting
- time and location of the meeting
- image of the ministry
- quality of the teaching
- opportunities for discussion
- opportunities for fellowship

Local Outreaches

An effective, growing ministry to single adults needs to have several outreach opportunities throughout the year. Single adults are, by necessity, self-centered at times. They are responsible for all of life's domestic, financial, and material tasks. Cooking, cleaning, laundry, car repairs, home repairs, yard work, running errands, paying bills, and all other chores are not shared by a spouse. Therefore single adults can become somewhat selfish out of necessity.

Opportunities for becoming involved in the lives of those who are less fortunate materially, emotionally, or physically help single adults to focus less on themselves and more on others. Regular outreach events should be a part of a healthy single adult ministry. A few ideas for these include:

- park events
- nursing home visitation
- hospital visitation
- street witnessing
- feeding and clothing the homeless
- rescue mission or Salvation Army services
- other volunteer work

There are many benefits to outreach events. They help single adults to:

- look outside themselves to the needs of others
- put their own problems into proper perspective
- gain a larger perspective of others
- gain a better perspective of God's compassion
- develop greater compassion in their own life
- give the ministry more credibility

What the Church Needs to Learn

A common and continual frustration of many leaders in single adult ministry is that married adults, pastors, and others in the church do not understand their ministry. Just as a church should think through and clearly state its mission and purpose, the leaders of a ministry to single adults should think through, articulate, and be aware of how the ministry influences and affects the congregation.

Bill Flanagan suggests four principles that the leadership of a single adult ministry hopes a congregation will learn:[2]

1. *We want to raise the consciousness of the whole church of Jesus Christ to understand that singleness is natural and healthy.* One is not a half number; it is a whole number! The tendency for the evangelical church to be marriage and family focused leaves single adults feeling less than whole some, if not much, of the time. Rather than viewing single adults as people who need our help relationally (hoping they will get married and become whole, normal couples), the goal for the church is to understand that all of us need to learn from one another and can benefit from ministering to each other, whether single or married.

Single people have much to teach and offer to the total body of Christ. The church needs to understand and believe that unmarried, separated, divorced, and widowed people are not always less fortunate than married people. We need to be committed to modeling the truth that personal fulfillment and wholeness does not come from marriage but through relationship with Christ (Col. 2:10).

2. *We want to bring the entire congregation to a deeper understanding of marriage, divorce, and remarriage.* A congregation watching, interacting with, and learning from individuals in an active single adult ministry will learn more about the issues of unconditional fidelity and commitment in marriage than a congregation without a single adult ministry. They will better perceive and discern the meaning of volitional love and when and where to go for help in a marriage or in their personal life when things begin to fall apart. This is because an effective ministry to single adults deals with the many relevant issues of marriage, divorce, and remarriage. The learning and healing that take place in the lives of individuals is bound to influence others in the church, both married and single.

There will be many opportunities to put biblical teaching concerning grace, forgiveness, and wholeness into practice among believers in the church. Openness and nonjudgmental attitudes will have greater opportunity to be displayed because of the many single and single-again individuals who are part of the single adult ministry. The issues, realities, and biblical teaching concerning marriage, divorce, and remarriage will also have a greater opportunity to be portrayed and, indeed, need to be addressed because of the numbers of divorced and remarried individuals who are attracted to a ministry to single adults.

3. *We are totally committed to the integration of single adults into the whole life of the church.* One of the goals of a single adult ministry is to see them eventually involved in the total life of the church: singing in the choir or worship groups, playing an instrument, teaching children, ushering, serving on the greeting staff, serving on teams and committees, helping in the kitchen, and so forth.

Single adult ministry is not a stopping place; it is a resting place for people for a temporary period of time. After individuals have been nurtured and have grown spiritually and relationally, many of them serving in one way or another in the single adult ministry, most of them will move on into the whole life of the church. Many will find a place of ministry in the church, fulfilling the biblical mandate of becoming a servant.

This reality is difficult for the director or pastor to accept at first. Training leaders for ministry to single adults, then seeing them move into another ministry within eighteen months is a hard pill to swallow. This "sliding door" principle is healthy, however, because it allows single adults to continue their spiritual, relational, and ministry growth, and it helps the rest of the church become educated and informed about ministry to single adults.

4. *Single adult leaders need to understand that the predominant goal of the people in their ministry groups is to find and develop healthy relationships with males and females, usually with the hope that they will eventually marry.* As was stated earlier, healthy friendships and compatible relationships are probably the biggest need and desire of single adults. It is sad that many churches do not recognize they should be one of the main places where opportunities for these to form are given. With the single adult population approaching 50 percent of all adults in the nation, the church should take the opportunity to provide outlets for healthy friendships and relationships with the same and opposite sex to form in a loving, Christian atmosphere. A healthy single adult ministry is a perfect example of one such opportunity.

Again, as stated above, the principle of a "meat market" should be vocally discouraged and disapproved of in order that the beauty and reality of Christian love and acceptance will be displayed. This reality will illustrate a community similar to that of the early church, which the secular world looked at and said, "See how they love each other."

PART
THREE

Development of Single
Adult Ministry

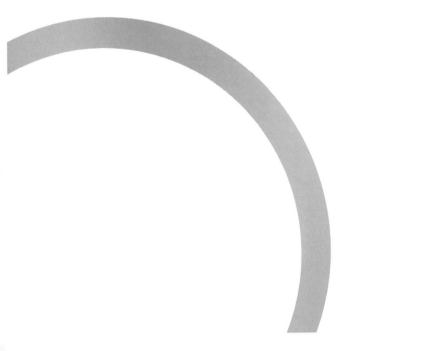

This section will address the challenge of beginning a ministry to and with single adults. The words *to and with* are used intentionally. A ministry designed for single and single-again adults is not only *to and for* them, but it is designed to be *with* them. In other words, it needs to be stressed that the individuals coming and participating in this ministry are adults, not children or teenagers. As adults, they will have the largest part in actually running the ministry. They have the time, talent, and creativity to minister to others in almost all facets of the ministry to be designed. Single adult ministry is truly one *to*, *for*, and *with* single adults.

Count the Cost—A Challenging Ministry

That being said, it is now imperative that church leaders count the cost before beginning this ministry. Luke 14:28 states, "Suppose one of you wants to build a tower. Will he not first sit down and estimate the cost to see if he has enough money to complete it?"

Simply stated, ministry to, for, and with single adults *is a challenging one!* Though it is not uncommon for leaders of any ministry to purport this claim, one will soon realize, given the vast age span (eighteen to sixty-five), various reasons for singleness (not yet married, divorced, widowed, single parent, separated), and the diversity of issues within the lives of single adults in each category, ministry to single adults encompasses almost *every personal issue and challenge in the church today*. It requires church leaders to make a determined commitment to reaching and ministering to a multiplicity of diverse individuals, many with complex and difficult issues. Ministry to single and single-again adults may stretch anyone spiritually, emotionally, physically, and relationally beyond what was expected or anticipated.

Count the Cost—A Rewarding Ministry

It should also be stressed, however, that *this ministry is one of great reward!* The rewards of ministry to and with single adults are numerous and deeply fulfilling. A few of them include:

- seeing individuals come to Christ as Savior and Lord
- seeing individuals set free from emotional bondages of fear, anger, and bitterness from a divorce or broken relationship
- helping people discover direction for their lives in career, relationships, finances, family issues, and so forth
- seeing people set free from addictions to alcohol, drugs, gambling, pornography, homosexuality, or fornication
- helping people grow spiritually, relationally, emotionally, and socially through involvement in ministry
- helping people discover their spiritual and ministry gifts and seeing them bless and assist individuals and the church
- seeing men and women establish healthy friendships and romantic relationships, some of them marrying
- reaping the personal and spiritual benefits of helping leaders network with other leaders, both inside and outside the church
- seeing healing and wholeness come through Christian fellowship and friendship

Single adult ministry requires leaders to count the cost, determining the answers to many key elements before deciding to build and then actually beginning to build the ministry. The elements of why, who, what, where, when, and how of a ministry to single adults need to be discussed and planned. These elements contain many important issues relating to recruiting, training, motivating, and retaining leadership. The elements comprising and influencing this decision are addressed in this section in detail.

Objectives of This Section

The following objectives are presented and discussed in detail throughout chapters 9, 10, and 11.

1. *Acquaint and familiarize the reader with many of the challenges and decisions in beginning a ministry from scratch.* The text lists

many critical questions to ask and answer when beginning this ministry. These questions cut to the chase concerning motives, attitudes, and priorities of those responsible for the decision to launch the ministry. They are presented in a direct and thought-provoking manner in chapter 9.

Other issues including understanding the different ages and types of single adults, the three major groups of single adults by church status, the various models of ministry, and the decision of where to host the ministry need to be thought through, prayed about, and decided upon sometime before and during the start-up process of the ministry. These important understandings are critical and deserve specific prayer, discussion, and decision before launching the group(s).

The specific steps suggested in chapter 9 for beginning a ministry are not intended to be a formula for sure success. Rather, they are presented as guidelines for beginning. Additionally, ministry to single adults in the small church involves several different principles than in the large church. The principles and issues listed and described are relevant to this scenario and deserve understanding and attention.

2. *Provide the reader an understanding of the many variables in selecting a pastor/director for the ministry and explore the many areas of leadership development needed to build a ministry to single adults.* Effective, passionate leadership in single adult ministry is critical. The pastor/director is the crucial person to inspire ambitious leaders who will own the ministry and take responsibility for ministering to people and developing effective ministry opportunities. It is important that the right leader be appointed: someone with vision, passion, organizational skills, and spiritual maturity. This individual will recruit and train the leadership team, who will assist in developing a healthy, positive, growing ministry to and with single adults.

The leadership team will have tremendous influence on people who attend and on the ministry as a whole. *Leadership is influence!* The leadership team will affect the:

- *Image of the ministry*—A single adult ministry will attract both spiritually and emotionally healthy and unhealthy people. The leadership team can help to keep the image of the group positive and growing.
- *Direction of the ministry*—Leaders need to be involved in making the decisions regarding direction of the ministry. People will support what they help to create.
- *Problem-solving for the ministry*—The leadership team deserves to know and help solve problems that will arise. The awareness and training through discussion and teaching will bring direction from God, will allow the group to benefit from the collective wisdom of the leaders, and will provide answers to the challenges.
- *Attendance in the ministry*—A healthy, involved, visible leadership team will foster greater attendance and involvement by the rest of the people.
- *Effectiveness of the ministry*—Leaders, by their verbal and physical involvement, will contribute to the overall success and effectiveness of the ministry. They are desperately needed.

In short, maturing, passionate leadership is the main ingredient for ministry to single adults and to growing an effective ministry that reaches and retains people. The wise pastor/director will invest much time into recruiting and developing leaders to assist in ministry to single adults.

3. *Educate the reader in the art of growing the ministry by developing leadership teams and discovering relevant resources.* As the ministry grows in numbers and effectiveness, additional leaders and ministries will be needed to care for and develop people. Leaders will need to recruit teams to assist in the ministries they oversee. These opportunities for involvement will bring spiritual growth to the individuals who serve on teams. They will grow twice as fast as those who are not involved and will attract others who need to serve in some capacity in the ministry.

Leaders will come and go for many reasons: moving, marrying, accepting other involvement in the church, occasional weariness, and so forth. They will need to be replaced with new individuals who will accept the challenge of overseeing an area of ministry and recruiting new people to their teams. The pastor/director will need to be bold and adept at replacing leaders because of the responsibilities they carry and the expectations of the group. A healthy single adult ministry will have a courageous, faith-filled, visionary, proactive leader at the helm who will assume responsibility for recruiting and/or will work with other leaders to recruit qualified leadership when needed.

Relevant Resources

Resources that relate to the personal life issues of people and provide sound, biblical instruction and direction are crucial to the teaching and discussion times in single adult ministry. In the opinion of this author, relevant teaching and the opportunity for regular discussion are two of the three most important needs of single adults. The third need is the ongoing opportunity for fellowship and developing quality friendships with the same and opposite sex. The pastor/director and various leaders responsible for the teaching and discussion segments of the classes need to consider quality resources a priority. When understanding how critical these are to the spiritual and personal growth of single adults, leaders will take the task of searching for biblically sound and relevant resources seriously.

The pastor/director and others responsible for the teaching ministry will benefit greatly and learn much from the *diversity of resources available today*. One should not be hesitant to evaluate books, videos, digital materials, and other resources just because they are from a different church background or a publisher unknown to them. Church doctrine is not usually the topic of teaching in most single adult ministries across the country today. Consequently, using material from sources other than one's own church background should not be a problem. If doctrinal teaching is desired, single adults can attend other classes the church offers. Personal life issues should be the main focus of teaching. These issues include a myriad of topics and themes in the spiritual, relational, emotional, financial, mental, and physical areas.

9

Beginning a Ministry from Scratch

Objectives

1. List ten important questions that should be asked and answered before beginning to plan and build a ministry to single adults.
2. Cause the reader to evaluate three challenges relevant to beginning a ministry.
   a. Groups of single adults by age and need
   b. Various models of ministry
   c. Whether to host the ministry on or off the church grounds
3. List and understand single adults as three groups by church status.
4. Relate and explain the steps that should be taken in beginning a ministry.
5. Identify and explain issues of single adult ministry in the small church.
6. List and describe other issues that are pertinent to beginning a ministry.

Questions to Answer before You Begin

Doug Fagerstrom, former pastor with single adults at Calvary Church in Grand Rapids, Michigan, suggests ten key questions the church leadership needs to consider before beginning a ministry with single adults.[1] These questions address very important issues and identify motives, attitudes, and priorities of the church leadership toward this ministry. I would highly encourage discussion and resolution of them before embarking on this ministry endeavor.

1. Do we really know the needs of our singles, regardless of their age or status?
2. Are we forsaking the pain of some singles in order to protect the prestige of our church or some of our established programs?
3. Will our ministry with single adults be confined to a singles group, or will we need to begin growing into new areas of departmentalization and integration?
4. Is our primary mission to seek and save the lost (Luke 19:10) and make disciples (Matt. 28:19–20), or is it to house and maintain the believers already in the door? How will this answer affect our attitude toward and treatment of "unacceptable" lifestyles among our single adults?
5. Are we guilty of imposing the youth model of ministry on our single adults?
6. Are we considering a new form of ministry directed to the particular singles in our church, or are we trying to follow the model of another church's ministry built upon the needs of their singles?
7. Are we still hung up theologically with the divorce/remarriage issue and can't (or don't want to try to) resolve this conflict?
8. Are we operating from the premise that this "singles phenomenon" will pass in a few years?
9. Do we really conduct our ministry as if all believers are ministers (1 Cor. 3:5–9)? What are the implications of this with our single adults, even those previously married?

10. Is the focus of our ministry primarily on our programs or our people (1 Cor. 16:15)? Where is most of our time and energy expended?

Honest discussion of these questions with both single adults and key church leaders will help lay the groundwork for a healthy ministry with single adults.

Understanding Single Adults by Groups

From the very outset of discussion concerning reaching single adults, it will be helpful to identify, understand, and decide which of several groups of people you intend to target (see table 9).

These groups of young adults and single adults were discussed in chapter 4, "Understanding the Diverse Needs of Single Adults," and chapter 5, "Who Are Single Adults? A Look at the Five Types." The numbers or types of single adults in your church can easily be obtained through a churchwide survey or the church's database (see page 162).

In addition to considering the ages and types of single adults, there is another important way to think of these individuals: *by church status.* Understanding there are at least three distinct groups of single adults who can be identified and targeted by church status helps to more clearly focus on one's mission. There are single adults in your church, in other churches, and in no church.

Table 9   Single Adults by Groups

Groups by Age	Groups by Need
young adults 18 to 25 years	single parents and children (preschool, grades 1–3, grades 4–6, teens)
young adults 25 to 35 years	divorce care and children (preschool, grades 1–3, grades 4–6, teens)
single adults 30 years and older	widowed
single adults 55 years and older	

Beginning a Ministry from Scratch

In your church—Every church has some single adults. The important questions about them, however, are:

Who are they?
How many are there?
What are their ages?
What is their single status?

A church may already have a database containing this information. If not, a short, written survey will quickly identify all adults by age, marital or single status, number and ages of children, etc. (see page 162). This survey can be made available on two consecutive Sunday mornings (to try to obtain responses from most who call this their church), with adults asked to complete and return only one survey on either Sunday. Collecting this information is important because it will identify which age group or need group should be started first.

In other churches—It is estimated that only 20 percent of all churches of any denomination or theological persuasion have *any type of ministry for any group of single adults*. Why should single adults in the other 80 percent of churches not benefit from the love, fellowship, teaching, and personal growth that your ministry will bring to their lives? I am not advocating encouraging them to leave their home church. Rather, I am encouraging churches to think outside of their walls and structured ministry times so that single adults from other churches will have the option of attending a targeted ministry. Examples of such times could include Sunday school time, a weeknight evening, or weekend evenings. For eight years we hosted a ministry on Sunday mornings between 9:00 and 10:30 that attracted up to twenty-seven different church backgrounds. At 10:30, people left to go to their own church services (most services began at 10:45 or 11:00 a.m.) The smaller the city, the easier it is to host a ministry on Sunday mornings off the church grounds and allow single adults to still attend their home church.

In no church—There are hundreds, thousands, even millions of single adults across the country who are not in any church. The numbers and single status of these people in your community can usually be obtained through the county courthouse or census bureau. These individuals should be part of your intended market also. Creative, innovative, relevant ministry opportunities will be attractive to them if planned and developed with excellence. These are some of the people whom Christ had in mind when he said, "Go into all the world" (Mark 16:15).

Which Ministry Model Is Right for You?

There are several models of ministry being used today. As stated earlier, each of these has its own purposes and characteristics and emphasizes a particular type and style of ministry. Chapter 6 described these models in detail:

1. Outreach
2. Discipleship
3. Discussion
4. Educational
5. Small Group
6. Social/Recreational
7. Contemporary Service
8. Combination

It is both necessary and exciting to discuss and plan the model(s) that is right for you and to launch it based upon the investment of prayer, dialogue, and planning that went into the decision. It is worth the time spent in discussion and prayer to be able to feel confident you have chosen the best model(s) to pursue.

Hosting the Ministry on or off the Church Grounds

The importance of evaluating where the ministry should be held was stressed in chapter 6. A ministry event does not have to be held in the church building just because it is sponsored by a particular church or even several churches. I have intentionally held weekly, ongoing single adult ministry groups for years both on the church grounds and off the church grounds for specific reasons. The decision concerning where to host the ministry can and should be highly influenced by several factors:

- The *size of the church(es)* sponsoring the ministry—Small churches do not usually attract large numbers of single adults inside the church building.
- The *number of churches* sponsoring the ministry—The greater the number of churches sponsoring a ministry, the greater the possible opportunity for hosting the ministry in a neutral location.
- The *model(s) chosen* to use in developing the ministry.
- The *advantages and disadvantages* of hosting the ministry on or off the church grounds.

Consult chapter 6 for further information concerning hosting the ministry on or off the church grounds.

Building a Ministry from Scratch

Let's review. Leadership individuals need to pray about, evaluate, decide, and review the following information during the process of beginning a ministry. These five elements are paramount to the success of the ministry and should be affirmed during all steps of beginning the ministry.

- Ask and answer the "Questions to Answer before You Begin" concerning motives, attitudes, and priorities.
- Decide which age group(s) or need group(s) will be targeted.
- Decide which of the three church status groups will be targeted.
- Decide which model of ministry will be used first.
- Decide whether to host the ministry on or off the church grounds.

Now it is time to consider a step-by-step process for beginning the ministry. These suggested steps are not offered as a formula for sure success but are given as guidelines for beginning.

1. *Pray*—Without consistent, fervent, ongoing prayer by potential leadership, the ministry will probably fail.
2. *Obtain permission and support*—Ask the senior pastor of the church for permission to begin this ministry. Without the support of the pastor, the ministry will struggle. The pastor needs to be involved in the birthing of this ministry, at the very least through determining direction, by undergirding it in prayer, and through personal support.
3. *Determine the demographics in your church*—If there is no information available concerning the demographics of your church, take a written survey in the church's main services. Page 162 provides an example of a survey. Poll your congregation on two consecutive Sundays (asking that each adult over the age of eighteen complete the survey only once) to determine the adult demographics of your church. Have people complete and turn it in during the service to ensure a good participation and return. Don't allow them to take it home to complete it! Most will not return it.
4. *Analyze the demographics/survey*—After you have taken the survey, tabulate the results in a form such as the example in table 10. This will give you a clear picture of the marital status and demographics of your church.
5. *Determine the demographics in your community*—Contact the county courthouse for demographic information of your town, city, or county community. You may also be able to obtain this information online from the census bureau.
6. *Decide or review which age and need group(s) you are beginning with and the reasons why they are being targeted*—If the church survey shows a larger percentage of single adults in the eighteen- to thirty-five-year-old range, perhaps it would be wise to begin a ministry to them first. I would call this ministry a "young adult" ministry. If the over thirty-five age group is larger, then perhaps that age group should be addressed first. If there are a large number of single parents, perhaps that group should be organized first. The leader of the group should be in the approximate age range of people the ministry is designed to

Adult Congregational Survey

Name: _____ Date: _____

Address: _____

_____

City: _____ State: _____ ZIP: _____

Home phone: (_____) _____ Cell phone: (_____) _____

Fax: (_____)_____ Email: _____

_____ Male   _____ Female

_____ Never Married   _____ Formerly Married   _____ Separated

_____ Married   _____ Widowed   _____ Single Parent   _____ Remarried

Your age:

_____ 18–25   _____ 26–35   _____ 36–45

_____ 46–55   _____ 56–65   _____ 66–75   _____ 76+

Names and ages of children at home under age 18:

_____   _____

_____   _____

_____   _____

_____   _____

_____   _____

_____   _____

Table 10   Demographic Summary

Age	M	F	Total Persons	Never Married	Married	Remarried	Formerly Married	Separated	Single Parent	Widowed
18–25										
26–35										
36–45										
46–55										
56–65										
66–75										
76+										

reach. Age and marital status of the leader will be discussed in chapter 10.

7. *Develop a contact list*—From the survey or church database, compile a contact list (address, email, phone) of single adults in the target age group or need group to be able to correspond regularly with them concerning directions, events, plans, etc.

8. *Organize planning meetings*—Gather a team of interested single men and women representing the targeted age or need group(s) to brainstorm and plan. Share the current ideas concerning type of group, model of ministry, on or off church grounds location, etc., for discussion and affirmation. Discuss possible meeting days, times, locations, teachers, and names for the ministry.

9. *Develop a mission statement and goals*—A mission statement represents the purpose of the ministry in a nutshell. This

should be developed early in the process to guide the direction of the group.

10. *Plan and host a large event*—Plan a large event designed to attract many single adults in the target age or need group. Take plenty of time (two to three months) to pray, plan, and promote the event before actually having it. Examples of events could include a retreat, conference, banquet, or social activity. Share the vision and potential plans for the ministry at the event.

11. *Name the ministry*—The leader(s) should pray, brainstorm, and decide on a name for the ministry. A name should represent:
    - the target age or need group
    - a positive image or meaning
    - a Christian image or meaning

12. *Hold the first class/session*—Begin the ministry by having the first class or session. Plan the class to be a weekly meeting on the same day, time, and location for clarity, convenience, and consistency.

13. *Begin weekly meetings*—It is important that momentum and regular opportunities for building friendships be established. Meeting only biweekly or monthly will not fulfill these needs as well as a weekly time.

14. *Establish a leadership team*—Look for and recruit adults who are interested in and passionate about this ministry. These people might be willing to accept a role of responsibility and appropriate authority needed to fulfill that role. Examples of areas needing leadership at this point could include: hospitality, follow-up, social activities, audio/visual, music, and discussion leaders. More concerning leadership will be addressed in chapter 10.

15. *Develop a balanced ministry*—A multifaceted ministry should be developed over a long period of time. Ministries addressing the six areas of life (spiritual, relational, social, physical, mental, emotional) should be planned. See chapter 7 for more information on these areas.

Ministry Issues in the Small Church

There are several issues in a small church that affect ministry to single adults differently than in a large church. Some of these include:

1. *Fewer single adults*—Smaller churches will have fewer single adults than larger churches. For example, a church of two hundred may have fifteen to twenty-five single adults of any age or type. It would be unwise to try to group all of them together every week in a ministry group. Younger adults in their twenties and thirties would soon leave if they are grouped with people their parents' and grandparents' ages. Different interests, physical abilities, and social desires due to different life stages would be apparent. Leaders in a small church need to decide which *one age group* they will target. A small church can only effectively reach one age group, unless it joins with at least one other church to cosponsor the ministry.

2. *Cosponsoring a ministry*—The day of the "Lone Ranger ministry" is over! Even a large single adult ministry needs to network with other ministries for expanding their vision, fellowship, and large events. *Small churches*, especially in small towns, *should consider joining together* to sponsor an area-wide ministry to single adults. In this way, there will be a larger pool of adults to draw from who will support the ministry. This breeds success, since single adults want to meet other single adults. Leaders may want to decide to host the regular weekly group at a neutral location, rather than in any of the church buildings. See chapter 6 for benefits, elements to consider, and room ideas. When considering cosponsorship, elements to resolve include:

   Finances—Issues regarding income, expenses, offerings, and checking accounts will need to be resolved.

   Meeting days and times—Avoid days and times that conflict with major services or events of any of the sponsoring churches.

Doctrine—Even though leaders of single adult ministries do not usually teach doctrine, pastors will want to have commonalities in this area.

Promotion of sponsoring churches—Pastors may want to agree on how and when each church will be promoted.

Leadership team—It would be wise, as much as possible, to have approximately equal numbers of individuals from each church on the leadership team.

3. *The volunteer leader*—Small churches are usually not able to hire a part-time or full-time person to develop the ministry as easily as large churches, so small churches usually have a volunteer leader. Large churches tend to be more aware of the numbers of single and single-again people because of their larger church body and tend to have a staff pastor to oversee the ministry. Having a volunteer leader is certainly better than having none at all, but the issues this person will have to deal with are many. Examples of these include possible lack of time, finances, networking relationships, training, and resources.

Lack of time—The volunteer leader will face the struggle of finding enough time to meet the demands of the ministry. Administration, planning, studying, teaching, recruiting and training leadership, finding resources, visitation, etc., take a lot of time. The volunteer leader needs financial, moral, and prayer support from the pastor and church leadership to be effective.

Lack of finances—Money to run the ministry will usually be in short supply in small churches and in many large churches also. Priority is usually given to the more traditional, established ministries of children, youth, and music before single adult ministry. Regular offerings should be taken and kept toward the expenses.

Networking relationships with other leaders—The volunteer leader needs to work diligently to find and develop relationships with other leaders of ministries in the same geographical area. Doing this as a volunteer leader may be more difficult than it would be for a paid staff person.

Teaching and training resources—Because small churches do not usually hire a leader for this ministry, they should, at the very minimum, pay for books, videos, and other teaching and training resources the leader will need. The leader should not hesitate or feel guilty about asking for this, realizing that most churches purchase curriculum and materials for children's, youth, music, and other ministries.

Other Issues Pertinent to Beginning a Ministry

Inform the senior pastor and church leaders regularly. At least during the first year the leader, or part of the leadership team, should meet regularly (about every four months) with the senior pastor to inform, educate, seek counsel, and pray together regarding the single adult ministry. This increases the opportunity for support and understanding and will greatly assist in building and developing the group(s). Ideas for obtaining continuing support include:

- Continually supply materials to the pastor to educate and inform him or her concerning your ministry.
- Ask for financial, promotional, prayer, and moral support.
- Feature the pastor at an upcoming major event to increase the pastor's understanding of your ministry.
- Interview church board members concerning their family and role in the church at a single adults meeting or class to increase their understanding of the ministry.
- Interview other staff pastors or ask them to speak at one of your meetings.
- Send mail, newsletters, and email to these church leaders.
- Talk with church leaders at church events regarding the single adults ministry.

Correct the congregational misconceptions. There are several misconceptions concerning single adult ministry that may arise and occasionally be voiced. Examples of these include:

dating market—a place to excessively look at the opposite sex
lonely hearts club—a place for lonely people to go
hospital—a place for the hurting, loser types to go
church—a place for people to go without being part of the larger body

These biases express what some individuals perceive a ministry to single adults to be. When verbalized, they tend to discourage some people from attending. Discuss these misconceptions both on the leadership team and in the ministry group for ideas regarding resolving and changing them (see chapter 8 for more information).

Include the ministry in the church budget. Any ministry worth having is worth funding. Becoming a part of the church budget is the goal. This is not always possible the first year, however, due to other ministry priorities of the pastor or church leadership. If this is the case, the following suggestions may be helpful.

- Continue to educate the pastor and church leadership concerning the financial needs of the ministry. Give examples of associated costs (such as postage, promotion, printing, honorariums, and supplies).
- Receive and retain offerings toward the expenses of the ministry. Realize that single adults will give to the cause if their needs are being met.
- Report ministry expenses to the church to demonstrate actual expenses and educate the leadership.
- Continue asking to be part of the church budget. Beginning with a small amount of subsidy one year is better than beginning every year with no amount of subsidy.

Promote the ministry regularly and enthusiastically. Promote your ministry consistently inside and outside of the church building.

There may be single adults who are new to the church and are looking for fellowship. There are also many single adults in the community who are not in any church regularly. Ideas for promotion include:

  inside the church—flyers, bulletins, dramas, posters, videos, emails, and visits to other classes and groups

  outside the church—websites, posters, ministry business cards, free newspaper advertisements, free radio announcements, and brochures in counseling offices and shopping centers

Word of mouth will prove to be one of the most effective means of promotion. If the ministry is effective and is meeting needs, people will be the best promoters.

Provide relevant teaching. It may seem unnecessary to mention this, but it is often overlooked when beginning a ministry. As stated in chapter 4, meeting the spiritual needs of individuals is certainly one of the top priorities of most churches across the country. The personal, topical needs, however, should not be overlooked. Most churches are doing an adequate job of addressing the spiritual needs of single adults through teaching, preaching, and small groups. They are *failing miserably*, however, in addressing the *personal, topical needs* from a biblical and single adult perspective. Providing teaching and discussion opportunities concerning relevant issues for single adults is one of the principle reasons for having this ministry. Issues such as sexuality and singleness, healthy friendships with the same and opposite sex, single parenting, divorce recovery, forgiving my ex-spouse, dealing with grief from loss of a spouse, dating or dating again, and many others need to be taught and discussed. For a complete list of topics, see chapter 4.

Plan community outreaches. Any ministry to single adults can easily become self-centered and inwardly focused. This is because of the necessity of single adults providing for all their own needs and because of the tendency for many individuals to come to the ministry while they are in some kind of crisis (spiritual, marital, relational, financial, or physical). Consequently, a wise leader or leadership team will plan occasional local outreach opportunities for single adults to become involved in (nursing home visitation, services at the Salvation Army, ministry to the homeless, or other area opportunities). These outreaches can help single adults to look outside of themselves, give them a greater understanding of others, give them a better, more positive perspective on life, give them a greater appreciation for what they have, and give your ministry credibility.

Opportunities to report to the entire church should be pursued because *nothing will change a negative ministry image to a positive one faster* than a church hearing how single adults ministered to those less fortunate.

10

The Pastor/Director and Basic Leadership Needed

Objectives

1. Identify and explain six levels of sensitivity to single adults shown by churches and the approaches churches take toward ministry to them.
2. Discuss the title and function of the pastor/director.
3. Define and describe three crucial roles of the pastor/director.
4. Emphasize four ministry principles pertinent to all leadership and show the advantages of appointing versus electing leaders.
5. Relate principles for recruiting leaders and qualities to look for and show an example of a leadership application.
6. Discuss the issues of males versus females and married adults versus single adults in leadership.
7. Identify basic leadership needed when beginning a ministry.
8. List reasons and benefits of using job descriptions and provide an example.

Church Levels of Sensitivity to Single Adults

There are at least six levels of sensitivity and approaches a church could have toward ministry to single adults:

Level 1. *No sensitivity or ministry to single adults*—This church and its leadership see no relevance or need for a targeted ministry to single adults, and they neither understand nor practice any intentional sensitivity toward them in the church's teaching, preaching, or programs. They may not be aware of their biases toward married adults, which are seen in event costs for single adults that are more than half the cost for married adults, insensitivity in teaching and preaching, lack of any financial or other help for single parents, etc.

Level 2. *Some sensitivity to single adults, but no targeted ministry to them*—This church and its leadership have only a little understanding of the needs and issues of single adults. There is no targeted ministry to single adults of any age, however.

Level 3. *More sensitivity to single adults, a targeted ministry, and a volunteer leader*—This church and its leadership may have more understanding of the needs of the various types of single adults than level 2 and may have appointed a volunteer leader to develop a ministry for them. In some cases, the church may wish the leader could be paid but for now can only support this person through prayer and material resources. This church may also display an understanding of the needs of single adults through care, concern, and consideration shown by inclusive words and phrases in preaching and teaching, equitable costs for events that do not show a bias toward married adults, provision of child care and help for single parents, and inclusion of single adults in some facets of leadership levels of the church.

Level 4. *Much sensitivity to single adults, a targeted ministry, and a part-time, paid leader*—This church and its leadership may have an even greater understanding of single adults than level 3 and show financial priority by budgeting for a part-time leader to develop and oversee the ministry. The leadership may be open to learning about and including single adults in all facets of the church, and they display an understanding of the needs of single adults through sensitivity in preaching and teaching, costs for events and programs, and other ways listed in level 3.

Level 5. *Much sensitivity to single adults, a targeted ministry, and a full-time staff member who has the single adult ministry as well as other ministries to develop*—This church and its leadership probably have a reasonably good understanding of single adults (or at least are open to learning) and may genuinely want to minister to them and see them become part of every area and leadership level of the church. Their understanding and openness may be displayed through sensitive preaching, teaching, and unbiased programs of the church as in level 4.

Level 6. *Much sensitivity to single adults, a targeted (often multifaceted) ministry, and a full-time, paid leader exclusively for single adult ministry*—This church and its leadership may have the greatest understanding of single adults (or at least are very open to learning), and they have hired a full-time person to develop and oversee the ministry. They are probably desirous of single adults becoming a part of every area and leadership level of the church. They may also display a greater understanding of and sensitivity to the needs and issues of single adults than most other levels due to the education they have received from the single adult minister and the single adults themselves.

These six approaches to single adults and appointing a leader to develop the ministry are influenced by a variety of factors including:

- the church's attitude and history of any prior ministry to single adults
- priorities of the pastor
- priorities of the board
- personal experience of the pastor(s) with single adults (in the church, community, work, immediate or extended family, etc.)
- the understanding and attitude of other leaders in the church

- budget concerns and priorities
- available potential leadership
- personal experience of the board with single adults
- personal experience of the staff with single adults
- personal experience of the congregation with single adults
- biases and verbal reactions and recommendations of the pastors, board, and congregation
- strength of ministries to single adults in other churches within the community
- number and type of existing ministries to single adults in the community and other churches
- size of the church

The Pastor/Director of the Ministry

The leader of the ministry will be the person the church looks to concerning vision for and development of the ministry to single adults. The leader's title may be different from church to church: pastor, director, leader, coordinator, facilitator, president, or some other title may be used. This person may also have a variety of tasks, but at the very least he or she will fill the role of a servant and should fulfill the following functions:[1]

1. Provide vision and direction for the ministry.
2. Recruit needed leaders and assist leaders in recruiting helpers.
3. Guide the leadership team in planning, implementing, and evaluating aspects of the ministry.
4. Define and endeavor to obtain resources, equipment, and supplies needed by the ministry.
5. Assist the leadership team in setting goals.
6. Train and motivate the leadership team.
7. Coordinate the beginning of new ministries.
8. Network with leaders of other ministries.

9. Serve as a liaison between the leadership team and church leaders.
10. Serve as a model for the leadership team.
11. Be responsible for the program, finances, and activities.
12. Take a personal interest in and minister to the leadership team.

The pastor/director of the single adult ministry is extremely critical to the effectiveness of the ministry and personal and spiritual growth of the people who will be a part of the group(s). Consequently, the leader should consider his or her main roles in leading the ministry. Three key roles this person will fulfill include:

1. *Dreamer*—The pastor/director of the ministry will need to be a dreamer. This person will be responsible for the overall vision of the ministry and will be accountable to God and the church leadership for fulfilling it. This person, possibly with the help of a small team of interested individuals, will need to answer the following questions:

• What does God want this ministry to become?
• What does the church leadership want this ministry to become?
• What gifts has God given me that will contribute to this vision?
• What type of leaders do I need to recruit and train to help fulfill this vision?
• What should this ministry look like in one year, three years, five years?
• Who else should we enlist for developing this ministry?

The pastor/director will need to communicate the vision and answers to these questions to the senior pastor, church board, and ministry leaders to be developed, and to encourage their support through prayer and participation at some level.

2. *Delegator*—The pastor/director of the ministry will need to be a delegator. It is imperative to understand that not all the deci-

The Pastor/Director and Basic Leadership Needed

sions of the ministry should be made by this one individual. Well-chosen ministry leaders will buy into the vision of the pastor/director and will more actively support what they have helped to create. When single adult leaders are allowed to make many of the decisions themselves and are directly involved in creating and running the ministry, they will grow personally, and the ministry will be strengthened. Delegation is a key to growing and developing the ministry and the personal lives of the leaders who assist in running it.

The pastor/director also should understand the following basic principles of authority. This leader is entrusted with the responsibility of developing the ministry to single adults, and consequently he or she needs to portray the following four elements regarding authority:

Accept it—Accept the authority given and do not run to the senior pastor or other superior for unnecessary decisions.

Give it—Give authority within proper limits to the leaders who will be recruited. Responsibility without authority is puppetry!

Teach it—Help leaders accept authority graciously and handle it wisely.

Model it—Model authority humbly.

3. *Discipler*—The pastor/director of the ministry needs to be a discipler. There is nothing more fulfilling than helping people grow spiritually, relationally, emotionally, and socially. The pastor/director will be the key individual in this process and will play an integral role in other leaders' lives. Simply stated, the pastor/director, as well as other leaders, will be a people builder and team builder. The following elements of training and motivating are relevant to both personal and team leadership development:

- pray together
- plan together

- play together
- problem-solve together
- dream together
- communicate the vision
- encourage
- motivate
- teach
- model transparency, honesty, and integrity

Ministry Principles Pertinent to All Leaders

Just as ministry to children, youth, senior adults, or any other targeted group in the church needs a leadership team, so does the ministry to single adults. One person cannot effectively fully develop a multifaceted ministry. Even if this were possible, the *people would be robbed of the opportunity for personal growth, fulfillment, and joy that comes through ownership of and involvement in the ministry*! It is extremely important that single adults be recruited, trained, and motivated to oversee most aspects of the ministry. Four simple, yet profound principles need to be stressed during the recruitment and training of leaders.

1. *Ownership*—Single adults need and deserve to own the ministry. It is not the pastor's/director's ministry; it is the people's ministry! This has been quoted before, but deserves quoting again. "People will support what they help to create." *Allow single adults to plan and run the ministry.* The job of the pastor/director is to give the ministry away, not to make all the decisions.
2. *Responsibility*—Leaders should be given specific responsibilities that are relevant to the total ministry. The ministry should be organized by the director and the leadership team and should fulfill the vision and mission statements. Trust the individuals recruited to fulfill their assigned tasks and develop their ministry areas. Leaders should consider them-

selves servants in the Lord's work, fulfilling specific needs of the body (Rom. 12:3–11; 1 Cor. 12).

3. *Accountability*—Help leaders to see that just as the pastor/director is accountable to a superior, they are also accountable to the pastor/director of the ministry. Accountability is a safety net for mistakes and an opportunity for forgiveness and modeling to take place. It provides a system of healthy checks and balances.

4. *Authority*—Appropriate authority (within limits) should be given to each leader. One of the *greatest mistakes I made* as a relatively new minister with single adults was *to give responsibility without giving authority!* Allow me to state it once again: *responsibility without authority is puppetry!*

The pastor/director needs to allow the leaders to make plans and decisions regarding their individual areas of ministry and not offer unsolicited advice. If leaders are given the freedom to make their own mistakes, they will learn from their mistakes and successes. I will never forget the lesson I learned from one of the pastors I served under early in my ministry. During the first month he called me into his office and said, "Dennis, I want you to make three good mistakes every month this year."

I gasped in surprised unbelief and replied, "Pastor, I thought you wanted me to succeed here, not make mistakes!"

He wisely retorted, "I do want you to be effective and succeed. But I also want you to try new things. Some of those will fail, and some of those new ideas will succeed. In other words, Dennis, you have the freedom to fail." I learned a great lesson that day. To succeed, one must first have the freedom to fail!

Appointing versus Electing Leaders

When the leadership of various churches began to develop single adult ministry in the mid- and late 1970s, it was common to allow single adults to elect their own leaders for the needed ministry positions. By the mid-1980s the general consensus among most single adult ministry leadership was that it was better to appoint rather than elect leaders. The reasons for this were fairly apparent.

1. More control over who fills the ministry position
2. More opportunity to obtain a person with gifts suitable for the ministry position
3. More opportunity to obtain a person with passion for the ministry position
4. More opportunity to obtain a person whose vision is compatible with that of the pastor/director
5. More flexibility of timing in obtaining the person
6. Less opportunity for a popularity contest because of voting

Appointment, rather than election, is now accepted and practiced across the country in most single adult ministries regardless of church affiliation.

Males versus Females in Leadership

The issue of men versus women in leadership should be discussed from two perspectives: the position of pastor/director of the single adult ministry and the members of the leadership team.

Pastor/director—Both women and men can be excellent leaders. There are effective ministries across the country led by women, and there are also effective ministries led by men. The philosophy of the senior pastor and church board regarding women in leadership may have an influence in selecting either a man or a woman for the position. The crucial need, however, is to appoint a person who will be a strong spiritual leader and can be effective in developing other leaders to help build the ministry.

At the risk of sounding one-sided or too general, here are some basic principles regarding the gender of the pastor/director:

• Men will usually attract and retain both genders better than women, especially for groups targeting people thirty-five years of age and older. This is because men born in the 1960s or earlier were raised to appreciate and be more comfortable with men than women in visible leadership positions.

- The smaller the church or ministry, the more significance the leader's gender may carry in beginning the ministry.
- Women usually have more organizational skills than men.
- Men may be perceived as having more spiritual authority than women.
- Leaders should be of the same approximate age as the target age of the ministry. If the target age is eighteen to twenty I would recommend a leader in the twenties or thirties. If the target age is thirty to thirty-five, I would recommend a leader in the forty to fifty year range.

Leadership team—These same general principles apply when selecting men and women for the leadership team. I would also add these additional principles:

- Older men (thirty-five and above) want to see men in leadership, especially in up-front roles. Jim Smoke, whom some consider to be the grandfather of single adult ministry, states, "If you have strong leaders—men or women—you will have men involved because men respect strength of leadership. However, I think it's important to remember that men will not come (as easily) if the ministry is mostly run by women. There must be men in visible areas of leadership."[2]
- Men and women on the leadership team will learn from each other, and their strengths will compliment each other's strengths.
- Generally, the older the group's age, the more *important, but difficult* it is to find male leadership. This principle makes it important for the pastor/director to work diligently at finding men to be in leadership.
- Many men in the boomer age category (born 1946–1964) may have more trouble following a female leader than those in the buster age category (born 1965–1982). The older the man, the more likely he may be to have grown up in an age dominated by men in leadership.

Married Adults versus Single Adults in Leadership

Both married adults and single adults can serve as effective leaders in single adult ministry. There are a few principles worth mentioning, however, that can serve as guidelines when considering married adults for either the pastor/director or the leadership team.

- Leaders, whether married or single, must demonstrate a passion for the people and ministry. A mere figurehead will not suffice! Single adults want and need leaders who show genuine interest and care for them.
- Younger age groups (under age thirty-five) are more accepting of *married couples* in leadership. Young adults do not identify themselves by their marital status as easily as older single adults. Therefore, young single adults seem to relate well to young married adults of approximately the same age.
- Older age groups (over age thirty-five) are more accepting of *remarried couples* in leadership. Remarried adults understand the needs and issues of the single-again person because they used to be single-again themselves. People who are single-again, either by death of a spouse or death of a marriage, will be the predominant type attending groups targeting those over thirty-five years old.

It is my contention that the leadership team should be *primarily single adults*. If the team is dominated by married adults, the single adults may be hesitant to serve in leadership. Single adults should be the majority on the leadership team because of:

- Life experiences
- Flexibility of time
- Understanding of single adult issues
- Respect of peers
- Example of life, growth, and maturity
- Identity of the ministry

The Pastor/Director and Basic Leadership Needed

Basic Leadership Needed When Beginning a Ministry

Leadership required for beginning a ministry can vary greatly depending on what type of group is being launched. The suggestions below are for the most common type of ministry to single adults and young adults, specifically an age-appropriate group with a weekly class or meeting (young adults ages eighteen to twenty-five, young adults in their midtwenties and thirties, single adults ages thirty and older, single adults ages fifty and older, etc.). For such a group, the following leadership/ministry positions should be appointed during the first year:

teacher—responsible for the teaching topics and teaching time

hospitality director—responsible for the greeting, staff nametags, and hosting staff

follow-up director—responsible for the staff who follow up with visitors and others who have been absent from the group for a number of weeks

music director—responsible for the vocal and instrumental music

discussion leader director—responsible for the staff of discussion leaders

refreshments director—responsible for the staff who provide food and beverages at the weekly class or meeting

activities director—responsible for the staff who plan and run the social and recreational activities

Principles for Recruiting Leaders

The person(s) responsible for recruiting leadership for the ministry could be one or more of the following: the pastor/director, an administrator of the ministry, the current leader of a specific ministry area, or a department coordinator within the ministry who oversees several leaders. Whoever is responsible for recruiting potential leaders, however, should be aware of some basic principles.

1. Know what skills are needed.
2. Seek God for guidance in selecting the right person.

3. Look for strengths in people who might fit the need.
4. Develop a relationship with potential leaders before approaching them about a leadership position.
5. Interview potential leaders.
   a. Ask those being considered for the position about their interest.
   b. Ask them to complete an application and return it by a specific date.
   c. After reviewing the application, if there is interest in the applicant, schedule a meeting. (A sample leadership application is provided at the end of this chapter.)
6. Explore the person's qualifications and desire for this area of leadership during the interview. Use the application as a guideline for discussion.
7. In her book *Single Adult Ministry for Today*, Bobbie Reed suggests several questions to ask the applicant.[3]

   - Why are you interested in a leadership position at this time?
   - What experiences have you had that enable you to be an effective team leader in our ministry?
   - Describe your leadership style and approach.
   - What are your leadership gifts and strengths?
   - What experiences have you had as a member of a leadership team?
   - Describe your personal relationship with God.
   - Share a recent experience that helped you grow spiritually.
   - How much time could you devote each week to this ministry?
   - How would you hope to grow as a person through this leadership experience?
   - What else would you like to tell about yourself?

8. Once a person has been chosen, ask him or her to serve for a specific period of time. This allows for a beginning and ending of the commitment, avoids causing the person to feel he or she

is in it for life, and gives the pastor/director an opportunity to appoint someone else in the future.

Basic Qualities to Look For in a Leader

There are many qualities that are desirable in a leader. Obviously no one person has them all, but it is important and helpful to know what skills and attitudes are needed, so you may look for a person possessing as many of these qualities as possible. It is also wise to seek the input of others concerning potential leaders. Others may recognize character traits in people that we do not see, and their comments could prove to be very insightful. Qualities to look for in potential leaders include:

- commitment to Christ
- action-oriented
- personable
- dependable
- faithful
- likeable
- growing
- balanced life (work, social, spiritual)
- desire to serve
- positive attitude
- able to accept authority
- able to delegate
- creative
- enthusiastic
- decisive
- patient

Using Job Descriptions

The church can learn a great deal from the secular world regarding leadership. One example of this is the use of job descriptions. An employer usually gives an employee a job description for several reasons, all of which are applicable in ministry also:

- People know what is expected of them.
- The pastor/director knows what to expect.
- It provides an opportunity for refinement and improvement of the job or the ministry.
- It provides an opportunity for refinement and improvement of the person.
- It provides an opportunity to maximize the amount of work accomplished.
- It gives clarity in explaining the ministry tasks when recruiting a team.

I believe it is important to give a job description to every ministry leader. The benefits of doing so are apparent. Following are two sample job descriptions (for many other sample job descriptions, visit the national single adult website of the Assemblies of God at www.singles .ag.org; click on Leaders/Ministry/Helps/Sample Job Descriptions):

Job Description—Activities Director

Purpose: The purpose of the Activities Director is to provide social/recreational activities for single adults that will promote fun and fellowship. This person is appointed by the pastor/director or his designated representative for a minimum period of six months and may serve a second term with permission.

Suggested Number of Volunteer Staff: two to four

Responsibilities:

1. Plan and implement one or two social activities each month. Activities for adults need to be varied. Activities used in the past include: dinners, camping, hiking, biking, swimming, banquets, tours, bowling, skating, parties, dinner theater, and other.

2. Recruit males and females to serve on the social team and help plan and hold social activities.
3. Publicize activities in advance. Contact the publicity director for posters and flyers or design them yourself. The church office can provide copies if needed. Bring flyers to the meetings and place on the tables.
4. Organization is a must! Planning must take place in advance of the event to ensure smoothness and effectiveness.
5. Establish and follow a refund policy. How long will you refund money? How many days before the event will you not refund money?
6. If renting a room, piece of equipment, etc., this must be cleared with the Minister to Single Adults.
7. If transportation is needed, request church vans as soon as possible through the office secretary or organize car pools.
8. The director is responsible for the complete organization of all social activities. This may include games, food, props, materials, decorations, printing of tickets, sales, etc.
9. The director should help ensure there will be no alcoholic beverages served, sold, or used at any single adult activity.
10. Complete an event preview detailing the following month's activities and give it to the newsletter director by the tenth of the preceding month for promotion in the newsletter.
11. Complete an event report following each event that has money involved. Give a copy to the pastor/director and retain one copy.
12. Arrange for someone to fulfill your responsibilities in your absence.
13. Give a two-week notice of resignation.
14. Serve as a member of the single adult staff and attend all meetings.
15. Lead regular social team meetings.

Job Description—Hospitality Director

Purpose: To help people feel welcome by giving love and care to every person through the hospitality ministry. This person is appointed by the Minister with Single Adults or a designated representative for a minimum period of six months. He/she may succeed himself/herself once with permission.

- Romans 12:13—Be given to hospitality
- Titus 1:8—Be a lover of hospitality
- 1 Peter 4:9—Use hospitality towards each other

Suggested Number of Volunteer Staff: four to eight

Responsibilities:

1. Recruit and motivate the greeting staff (one male and one female each week). Welcome everyone whether they are a regular attendee or a new attendee.
2. Provide a name tag to everyone. (First name in capital letters).
3. Have each visitor complete a welcome card (ask person to press hard). A. First Copy—Give to office. B. Second Copy—Give to Follow Up Director to give to host/hostesses. C. Third copy—Give to Follow Up Director to file.
4. Provide each visitor with a newsletter (if available) and any current brochures/flyers.
5. Maintain ample amounts of supplies (name tags, pens, storage materials, etc.)
6. Arrange for someone to fulfill your responsibilities in your absence.
7. Recruit and help train an assistant who could possibly replace you upon your resignation.
8. Serve as a member of the General Council and attend all leadership meetings.
9. Lead an occasional Hospitality Department meeting.
10. Give a two-week notice of resignation.
11. Attend the leadership class "Improving Your Serve."

Date Given: _____

Date Returned: _____

Sample DIRECTOR APPLICATION
SINGLE LIFE MINISTRIES/BETHEL CHURCH

Ministry Position Desired: _____ Date: _____

Department Coordinator for this Area of Ministry: _____

Coordinator Phone (HM): _____ Phone (WK): _____

Applicant: _____

Phone (HM): _____ Phone (WK): _____

Address: _____

City: _____ Zip Code: _____

D.O.B. _____ Email: _____

_____Never Married _____Formerly Married _____Widowed _____Separated

Do you have children? ___Yes ___No

If so, what are their names and ages? _____

_____

GENERAL INFORMATION

1) How long have you been attending Single Life Ministries? _____

2) How long have you been attending Bethel Church? _____

3) How did you hear about this ministry opportunity? (circle a, b, c, or d)
   a) Sunday school class, Spirited Singles, or TNT announcement
   b) Person in SLM Leadership recruited me
   c) Saw help-wanted ad in "Single Times"
   d) I asked around to see how I could help out

MINISTRY LIFE

1) Have you ever been involved in another helping ministry?
   ___Yes ___No

   Bethel or another church? _____

   What church? _____

2) What were your basic responsibilities? _____

_____

_____

3) How do you feel your abilities can be best used to help in this area of ministry? _____

_____

_____

_____

4) Have you ever worked with others on a project or event? _____

How do you feel about working with others as a team? _____

_____

_____

5) Check the word which best describes how you usually handle conflict with other people:

___Withdraw ___Compromise ___Yield ___Fight ___Resolve

6) Why do you think that this is a good time in your life to be involved in this ministry position? _____

_____

_____

_____

SPIRITUAL LIFE

Please answer briefly but adequately enough to convey your thoughts.

1) Have you received Jesus Christ as your personal savior? When? Please explain. _____

_____

_____

2) Briefly describe what your relationship with Christ means to you. _____

_____

_____

_____

3) How do you feel your involvement in this ministry will affect or enhance your relationship with Christ and others? _____

_____

_____

COMMITMENT

1) Would you be willing to attend the SLM "Improving Your Serve" Class (8 weeks) and make a minimum 6-month commitment to this ministry?

___Yes   ___No

If no, please explain: _____

_____

_____

Comments/Questions?

_____

_____

_____

_____

_____

_____

_____

_____

_____

_____

Thank you for your interest in serving as a Director in an SLM Ministry. The selection of leaders depends upon the ministries available, the number of applications, and the approval of the Executive Council. *Please return this application to the Department Coordinator or to the person who gave it to you.*

11

Forming Leadership Teams, Developing the Ministry, Finding Relevant Resources

Objectives

1. List and define principles for training the leadership team and show qualities leaders should possess.
2. List reasons and principles for helping leaders build their own teams and show a survey tool to help do this.
3. Suggest and explain relevant ways to motivate the leadership team(s).
4. List principles for retaining leaders.
5. Name various areas within the ministry that the main leadership team should evaluate.
6. Suggest additional leadership positions and organizational ideas for expanding and growing a ministry.
7. Explain the need for and list ideas for networking leaders with leaders from other single adult ministries in the community and state.

8. List resources in several categories that are pertinent to single adult ministry.

Principles for Training the Leadership Team

There is so much that could be written regarding training leadership. *I believe it is the key to an effective, growing ministry to single adults.* The leadership team will multiply the influence of the pastor/director, have great influence with their particular circle of friends, serve as role models for the group, and become key components in developing the ministry. Consequently, it is imperative that the pastor/director see developing leadership as a primary role. It is this person's job to recruit, train, and motivate the leadership team. If attention is not given to this responsibility, leaders will not grow and be as effective as they could be, and the ministry will suffer greatly.

Training new leaders is an ongoing process, especially in this ministry. Leadership turnover is a constant reality due to the "sliding door" principle (leaders fulfill their commitment, leave the ministry, and move into a different area of ministry involvement in the church). This is a very *common and needed* reality. It is a sign of health for single adults to move out of the ministry and into the larger life of the church; integration into the total life of the church is one of the goals of single adult ministry. These adults need to mix with other individuals who are younger, older, or married.

Basic training ideas for the leadership team include:

1. *Meet individually with key leaders on a regular basis.* This can be done over lunch or coffee to express a personal interest in them, solve problems, brainstorm, pray for them, and so forth.
2. *Meet with the leadership team on a regular basis.* The four "I-words" can be a good guideline to follow in planning for these meetings.

> *Information*—what needs to be told by the director and each leader?
> *Involvement*—what needs to be discussed?

Instruction—what needs to be taught for personal and ministry growth?

Inspiration—what needs to be shared for motivation?

3. *Give reading assignments.* Choose a leadership development book and ask the team to read a chapter and be prepared to discuss it at the next meeting.
4. *Teach and discuss leadership principles.* There are many good books that teach spiritual, organizational, and ministry leadership principles.
5. *Model transparency.* The pastor/director needs to live a transparent and genuine life in front of the leadership team as well as admit mistakes and weaknesses to the team.
6. *Hold a leadership class* once or twice a year for the purposes of:

   - discovering potential leaders
   - training existing leaders and potential leaders
   - building unity in the leadership team
   - imparting vision to existing and potential leaders
   - improving leadership skills
   - praying together
   - spiritual growth of the leaders

7. *Plan and host a leadership retreat once a year* for the same purposes as the leadership class but also to have fun together.
8. *Pray consistently and persistently.* The leadership team needs to be taught the dire importance of prayer, and their lives need to model an example of prayer for the rest of the group (2 Chron. 7:14). The larger the ministry, the more prayer is needed. Without prayer, the ministry will become mechanical and will lack effectiveness.

Qualities Leaders Should Possess

In his article "What Makes a Leader?" Warren Bennis lists eight qualities a leader possesses.[1] These qualities are based on a study of ninety top executives in both the public and private sectors, and they underscore the importance of leadership and its much-needed influence.

1. *They focus on doing the right things versus doing things right.* While most managers concern themselves with doing things right, leaders focus on doing the right things.
2. *They have a compelling vision and a dream for their work.* The passion of their work is motivating.
3. *They are the most results-oriented people I ever encountered.* They are highly conscious of what they want.
4. *They share an ability to communicate.* An effective leader has to be able to communicate ideas in a way that people can understand.
5. *They help their followers feel important.* Those who work with them feel significant and empowered.
6. *They are committed and persistent.* Leaders are able to hang in there and stay the course.
7. *They know their own worth; they have positive self-regard.* They realize what their strengths are and know how to nourish and nurture them.
8. *They don't think about failure; it's what I call the Wallenda factor.* Like Karl Wallenda, the tightrope walker, leaders put all their energy into walking the tightrope; they don't worry about possible failure. Though it is always a possibility, it should not dictate their efforts or actions.

Helping Leaders Build Their Own Teams

The principle of building teams needs to be stressed at this point. In many cases leaders will need to have helpers and possibly additional leaders to assist them in their ministries. It is best to allow the leaders themselves to recruit these individuals rather than the pastor/director appointing them. The leadership team should set guidelines for recruitment or appointment of additional staff before any recruitment begins. Also, individuals appointed to oversee a specific ministry area should be taught how to develop a team to minister with them and work together in community toward a common goal. This will help them learn important skills of praying for God's direction, building friendships, recruitment, working with others, developing unity, sharing the work, motivating others, etc.

The pastor/director should teach the other leaders how to recruit and motivate teams at regular leadership meetings (using the same principles listed above). The importance and benefits of building a team of helpers and other leaders needs to be stressed to the leaders as they build their teams. These include:

- sharing the work
- experiencing joy from serving
- personal growth of the leader
- less chance of burnout
- learning from others
- developing unity

Use a survey for finding helpers and other leaders (a sample survey tool is included at the end of this chapter). This allows others in the ministry to know where help is needed and to express interest in several areas. This survey could be given to a class or group two to three times per year, or used individually by leaders as often as needed to identify and recruit others. Leaders of each ministry area should be given the responsibility of following up on those who have expressed interest in particular areas.

Motivating the Leadership Team

It is also important to motivate the leadership team! Ministry to single adults can be extremely challenging, demanding much time, effort, and emotional investment from those in leadership. Encouragement from the pastor/director and from other leaders will contribute to a healthy leadership team. The excellent list below of leadership ideas for a pastor/director of a single adult ministry is provided by Bobbie Reed in an article entitled "How to Retain Single Adults in Leadership Positions."[2]

1. *Empower*—Allow the Holy Spirit to guide their ministry. Delegate the responsibility and authority commensurate with the task. Let leaders feel free to take risks, to try new strategies, and even sometimes to fail.
2. *Equip*—Ensure that leaders have the necessary skills, knowledge, and proper funding, supplies, and equipment to do their assigned task.
3. *Encourage*—Affirm your leaders. Let them know what they are doing well. When things don't go right, share an experience when you failed and reassure them that failure is something everyone experiences. Help them learn from failures.
4. *Recognize*—Be creative in the ways you recognize your leaders. Be quick to praise their successes. Give all due credit and recognize them in public.
5. *Reward*—Find ways to reward your leaders publicly. Give them tickets to a ball game or gift certificates for dinner at a restaurant. The rewards need not be expensive; the thought is what counts. The group needs to see and hear about the successes of the leadership.
6. *Relieve*—Don't recruit a leader for an indeterminate amount of time. Be clear when you first discuss the position that the commitment time is limited. Start with a short commitment—three months or a year at the most. They can reenlist at the end of the initial commitment.
7. *Listen*—Talk with your leaders frequently. Ask how things are going. Follow through on issues and concerns.
8. *Love*—People respond to love. If you truly care for your leaders as individuals, they will sense your concern and will consider you their friend in ministry.
9. *Learn*—Be willing to learn from those you recruit. Don't miss out on an idea simply because you are the pastor/director.
10. *Lead*—A genuine leader is more concerned with developing people than developing programs. A leader is a guide, a model, an encourager, and a supporter who helps strong people become true leaders.

Bobbie's suggestions are extremely insightful and helpful. I want to add only a few additional thoughts:

1. *Model faith, trust, and dependence on God.* The team needs to see the pastor/director asking and trusting God for direction and strength.
2. *Model enthusiasm and a positive outlook.* Single adult ministry is one of the most fun ministries in the church today!
3. *Model a good work ethic.* Work hard at what you do.
4. *Trust them to do the job they have accepted.* Micromanagement is unnecessary and breeds suspicion, frustration, and lack of trust.
5. *Correct them privately.* There is no wisdom in correcting a person in front of others. It causes humiliation and embarrassment.
6. *Model loyalty.* Be loyal to the team. Believe in them. Believe them first during conflict or accusation.
7. *Teach loyalty.* Leaders need to understand the importance of being loyal to the pastor/director and to the ministry.

There are four types of bones that illustrate four types of people. It's obvious which type of person is the most loyal, helpful, and teachable and would make a good leader.

Wishbone—"I wish our leader would do this . . . then I could really be supportive."

Jawbone—"I'll help you build this ministry" (but the person is lazy or apathetic and does not actually help).

Knucklebone—"If I was in charge I would change . . ." (knocking the way things are done).

Backbone—"I'll help you build this ministry" (and does).

Areas of Ministry Leaders Should Evaluate

An effective ministry to single adults will require periodic evaluation by the leadership team. Neither the pastor/director nor leaders themselves should be hesitant or afraid to give honest evaluation of these areas. Improvement and greater effectiveness will result from it. Both evaluation through discussion and written evaluation will prove extremely beneficial. Areas of evaluation could include:

- teaching topics—relevance, frequency, personal versus spiritual issues
- teachers—effectiveness, ideas for guests
- format of the class, including time allotment for each segment
- friendliness of the leaders toward guests
- friendliness of the group toward guests
- effectiveness of the current follow-up ministry of guests
- meeting room, day, time, length
- social activities—type, frequency, cost
- leadership meetings—frequency, effectiveness, time, length, potential leaders, ideas
- outreach ministries—frequency, type, ideas

Leadership for Growing and Expanding a Ministry

As the ministry grows, there may be a need to begin other groups or models such as other age groups, a single-parent family ministry, a divorce recovery ministry, or a widowed ministry. Each of these will require leadership to begin and develop them. The same principles for recruiting and training leaders should be used as stated earlier. Ideas for other leadership/ministry positions are almost limitless. Many of them are listed below:

- head usher
- audio/visual director
- Sunday lunch director
- sports director
- photography director
- video director

- newsletter director
- small groups director
- drama director
- outreach director
- prayer director
- emcee
- teachers
- benevolence director
- materials table director
- book/CD table director
- visual arts director
- publicity director
- children's groups director
- retreat director
- special events director
- seminar/workshop director
- life-share director (testimonies)

Establishing Departments within the Ministry

A multifaceted ministry for single adults and/or young adults may require setting up various major ministry departments to assist the pastor/director in overseeing the total ministry. Each department could have a coordinator and contain various ministry areas relevant to the department. Coordinators would meet as a team with the pastor/director on a regular basis. Each ministry area within a department would be overseen by leaders who are accountable to the department coordinator and would meet regularly as a team with their coordinator. For example, a ministry with two or more classes organized by age could consider them departments:

- Young Adult Department—ages eighteen to twenty-five
- Young Adult Department—ages twenty-six to thirty-five

- Single Adult Department—ages thirty and older
- Single Adult Department—ages fifty-five and older

Other departments in the ministry might include:

- Single-Parent Family Department
- Widowed-Care Department
- Divorce Recovery Workshop Department
- Newsletter Department
- Friday Night Live Department
- Local Outreaches Department
- Foreign Mission Trips Department

These departments could be started as the pastor/director and total leadership team discuss vision, timing, leadership, resources, facilities, cost, and materials. In this way the single adult ministry can become one that meets many of the diverse needs of single adults. It also encourages utilizing the talents, skills, and creativity of the people and allows God to further develop them. A diagram of sample departments and their leadership is included at the end of this chapter.

Networking with Leaders from Other Single Adult Ministries

Connecting your leadership team with leaders from other single adult ministries can be a healthy, motivating, learning experience. The days of the Lone Ranger ministry are far past! Leaders from your ministry *need to network with leaders from other ministries.* They will benefit from the relationships and fellowship with others in similar ministries, and they will receive a larger vision. Look for other ministries in your area and even outside your area if there are none close by. They do not need to be from the same church background or denomination; ministry to single adults will be the common denominator.

A few ideas for meeting and involving your leadership with leaders from other groups include:

- sponsor a leadership meeting
- sponsor a leadership retreat
- host a major social, recreational, or spiritual event together (such as a New Year's party, banquet, retreat, conference)
- host a speaker or video pertaining to leadership development
- host a prayer meeting for leaders of several groups
- host a lunch or dinner for all leaders

Resources for Ministry with Single Adults

Resources for ministry with single adults began to surface in the late 1970s as churches and leaders of many denominations and backgrounds became more aware of the vast numbers of single and single-again people in society and, to some extent, in the church. Pollsters, authors, and church leaders were seeing the permanence of several social revolutions: postponement of marriage, no fault divorce and resultant high divorce rates, remarriage, increasing single-parent families, etc. These all pointed to the fact that single adults were here to stay. It became apparent that to be effective in reaching and retaining single adults, an emphasis upon targeted ministry in the local church was needed.

At the end of this book there are lists of resources for single adult ministry, resources for leadership training and leadership development, and denominational offices for single adult/young adult ministries. These are not meant to be exhaustive, and one must realize they may change or go out of print at any time. They are listed as resource ideas for effective ministry to and with single adults and the leadership working with them. Doctrinal and theological perspectives may differ depending on the authors and publishers.

Survey to Enlist Helpers/Workers in a Ministry

Please check any areas of interest to you!

ACTIVITIES

____Planning Conferences/Retreats
____Planning Sunday Lunches
____Planning Special Events
____Planning Social Activities
____Refreshments/Food Preparation
____Planning Sports/Recreational Activities

AUDIO/VISUAL

____Sound, Overhead Projection, Taping
____Photographer
____Set-up (Tables, Chairs, Props)
____Video (Recording, Editing)

COMMUNICATIONS

____Book/Tapes
____Drama
____Materials Table
____Newsletter (Writing, Mailing, Design, Graphics, Printing)
____Publicity (Designing Flyers & Posters)

MUSIC

____Musical Accompaniment for Praise & Worship
    (Piano, Guitar, Drums, Bass Guitar, Etc.)
____Instrument You Play _____
    ____By Note ____By Ear
____Praise & Worship Leader
____Singing
    ____Solos ____Duet ____Group ____Melody ____Alto ____Tenor ____Bass

OUTREACH

____T.L.C. (Convalescent Visitation)
____Missions Trips (Puppets, Drama, Music)
____Street Light—Witnessing
____Homeless Ministry:
    ____Food ____Music ____Clothing ____Tracts
____Skills I could use to help others with Personal Needs:
    ____Carpentry ____Mechanics ____Sewing ____Painting ____Lawn Care
    ____Fix-Up ____Help with Moving ____Other _____

OTHER

____Office Help
____Monetary Help for Special Retreats, Events, & Projects
____Administration/Overseeing People & Projects
____Usher
____Van Driver for Activities

RELATIONSHIP RECOVERY WORKSHOP

____Group Discussion Facilitator
____Refreshments Help
____Teacher
____Giving a Short Testimony
____Decorations Help
____Registration

Departmental Organization Diagram

Activities Dept. Coordinator

A) Social Activities Director
B) Sports Activities Director

Just Me & the Kids Dept. Coordinator & Assistant Coordinator

A) Activities Director
B) Music Director
C) Hospitality Director
D) Follow-up Director
E) Refreshments Director

Divorce Recovery Dept. Coordinator (2)

A) Female Facilitators
B) Male Facilitators
C) Teachers
D) Refreshments
E) Nursery Workers
F) Children's Teachers

Outreach Dept. Coordinator

A) Street Light Director
B) Tender Loving Companions Director

Spiritual Growth Dept. Coordinator

A) Home Group Directors
B) Prayer Director

Wednesday Night Live Coordinator

A) Activities Director
B) Altar Workers Director
C) Audio/Visual Director
D) Band Director
E) Emcees
F) Follow-up Director
G) Head Usher
H) Hospitality Director—Hosts/Hostesses/Greeters
I) Prayer & Testimony Director
J) Refreshments Director
K) Special Music Director

Communications Dept. Coordinator

A) Audio/Visual Director
B) Bookshelf Director

C) Council Secretary
D) J.U.S.T. Drama Director
E) Materials/Music Library Director

Just Me & the Kids Children's Ministry Coordinator

A) Nursery Care
B) Seeds Director—Class Helpers
C) Sprouts Director—Class Helpers
D) Shoots Director—Class Helpers

Newsletter Dept. Managing Editor

A) Layout/Design Director
B) Mailing Director
C) Managing Editor
D) Writers

Spirited Singles Dept. Coordinator

A) Audio/Visual Director
B) Follow-up Director
C) Food Director
D) Head Usher
E) Hospitality Director
F) Music Director
G) Secretary

Sunday Dept. Coordinator (3)

A) Audio/Visual Director
B) Emcee
C) Follow-up Director
D) Get-A-Way Director
E) Head Usher
F) Hospitality Director—Hosts/Hostesses/Greeters
G) Music Director
H) Refreshments Director

Sunday Dept. Teacher (4)

A) Young Adults (24–29)
B) Single Focus (All Ages)
C) Grow with the Word (All Ages)
D) Single Spirit (50 & UP)

Notes

Introduction

1. Edward and Gwen Weising, *Singleness—An Opportunity for Growth and Fulfillment* (Springfield: Gospel Publishing House, 1981), 2.
2. U.S. Census Bureau, January 2000, http://www.census.gov/population/cen2000/phct27/tab04.pdf
3. Ibid.

Chapter 1

1. *New Catholic Encyclopedia*, s.vv. "Canon Law of Celibacy," "History of Celibacy," vol. 3, 366–74.
2. U.S. Census Bureau, January 2001.
3. Frank Stagg, "Biblical Perspectives on the Single Person," *Review and Expositor* 74 (Winter 1977): 7.
4. D. M. Spence and Joseph S. Excell, *The Pulpit Commentary*, vol. 19 (Grand Rapids: Eerdmans, 1950), 246.
5. Samuel R. Driver, Alfred Plummer, and Charles Briggs, *International Critical Commentary* (Edinburgh: Marion & Gibb, 1965), 200.
6. Xenophon *Cyropaedia* vii.5.60–65.
7. Driver, Plummer, and Briggs, *International Critical Commentary*, 201.
8. Philo of Alexandria *Hypothetica* 11.14, quoted in Stagg, "Biblical Perspectives on the Single Person," 9.
9. J. D. Douglas, *New Bible Dictionary* (Leicester, England: InterVarsity, 1962), 349.
10. Stagg, "Biblical Perspectives on the Single Person," 9.
11. Driver, Plummer, and Briggs, *International Critical Commentary*, 205.
12. Spence and Excell, *The Pulpit Commentary*, vol. 1, 246.
13. "Family," *Time*, September 25, 2000.

14. U.S. Census Bureau, January 2001.

15. William E. Phipps, "Did Jesus or Paul Marry?" quoted in Brian L. Harbour, *Famous Singles of the Bible* (Nashville: Broadman, 1980), 121.

16. Ibid., 122.

17. Ibid.

18. Ibid.,116.

19. Ibid., 119.

20. Ibid.

21. Stagg, "Biblical Perspectives on the Single Person," 15.

Chapter 2

1. Carolyn Koons, "Today's Single Adult Phenomenon: The Realities, Myths, and Identity," in *Baker Handbook of Single Adult Ministry*, ed. Douglas Fagerstrom (Grand Rapids: Baker, 1997), 18.

2. U.S. Census Bureau, January 2001, http://www.census.gov/population/cen2000/phc-t27/tob04.pdf.

3. U.S. Census Bureau, "Living Together, Living Alone: Families and Living Arrangements," http://www.census.gov/population/pop-profile/2000/chap05.pdf.

4. Susan Goter, "Nearly One Half of All U.S. Households Consist of Single Adults," *Single Adult Ministry Journal* 124 (1997): 4.

5. "Family," *Time*, September 25, 2000.

6. The National Marriage Project, Rutgers University, 1998.

7. U.S. Census Bureau, January 2001.

8. "Family," *Time*, September 25, 2000.

9. Jennifer Baker, when asked in an oral inteview 5/04.

10. The first three statistics are from Susan H. Greenberg and Anna Kutchment, "The 'Familymoon,' " *Newsweek*, Jan. 9, 2006, 2. The last two statistics are from E. Mavis Hetherington and John Kelly, *For Better or For Worse: Divorce Reconsidered* (London: W. W. Norton, 2002). Hetherington and Kelly specify the divorce rate for step-couples to be 50 percent higher in marriage with stepchildren. Specifically, then, the divorce rate is 65–70 percent.

11. George Barna, *Unmarried America: How Singles Are Changing and What It Means for the Church* (Glendale, CA: Barna Research Group, 1993), 22.

12. Rick Cole, senior pastor of Capital Christian Center, Sacramento, CA, when asked in a written interview "Why should a church minister to single adults?" September 19, 1999.

13. George Barna, *Single Focus: Understanding Single Adults* (Ventura, CA: Regal, 2003), 15.

14. Goter, "Nearly One Half," 7.

15. George Barna, *Single Adults* (Glendale, CA: Barna Research Group, 2002), 7.

16. Ibid., 17.

17. Ibid., 18.

18. Ibid.

19. Ibid., 20.

20. U.S. Census Bureau, January 2000, http://eire.census.gov/popest/archives/1990.php#household.

21. Ibid.

22. The National Marriage Project, Rutgers University, 1998.

23. Ibid.

24. Ibid.

25. Ibid.

26. Don Weston, "All About Cohabiting Before Marriage," 2001, http://members.aol.com/cohabiting, 3.

27. Pamela Paul, *The Starter Marriage and Future of Matrimony* (New York: Villard Books, Random House, 2002), 9.

28. Lyle Schaller, "You and Your Un-Churched Neighbor," *Lutheran Standard* (January 1985): 4–7.

29. Don Davidson, *How to Build an Exciting Singles Ministry* (Nashville: Thomas Nelson, 1993), 1.

30. David Reddout, Pastor of First Assembly of God, Leesville, LA, Adult Ministries Consultant, Assemblies of God Sunday School Department, 1981–1985.

31. Scott Nelson, single adult/young adult pastor, First Assembly of God, Fort Wayne, IN, personal email correspondence, May 22, 2003.

Chapter 3

1. Harold Ivan Smith, "Singles Ministry Cannot Be Ignored," in Jerry Jones's *Growing Your Single Adult Ministry* (Colorado Springs: Cook Communication Ministries, 1993), 18–19.

2. Ibid., 19.

3. Ibid.

4. Greg Davis, single adult leader in Castro Valley, California, personal email correspondence, May 6, 2003.

5. Helen Marispini, single adult leader, Livermore, California, personal phone interview, May 17, 2003.

6. Koons, "Today's Single Adult Phenomenon," in *Baker Handbook of Single Adult Ministry*, ed. Fagerstrom, 21.

7. Ibid.

8. "Who Receives Child Support?" U.S. Census Bureau, May 1995, http://www.census.gov.

9. "Most Single Female Custodial Parents Had Child Support Awards," U.S. Census Bureau, March 2000, http://www.census.gov.

10. Ibid.

Chapter 4

1. Fagerstrom, ed., *Baker Handbook of Single Adult Ministry*, 29.

2. Lisa Stevko, "Single Source," a ministry of Valley Christian Center, Dublin, California, 2000.

3. Barna, *Single Focus*, 15.

4. Bobbie Reed, "Developing Ministry to Single Parents," in *Baker Handbook of Single Adult Ministry*, ed. Fagerstrom, 325.

Chapter 5

1. U.S. Census Bureau, January 2001.
2. Ibid.
3. "Family," *Time*, September 25, 2000.
4. Barna, *Unmarried America*, 22.
5. Barna, *Single Adults*, 7, 18.
6. Susan Goter, "Nearly One Half of All U.S. Households Consist of Single Adults," *Single Adult Ministry Journal* 124, (1997): 7.
7. Wade F. Horn, president of the National Fatherhood Initiative, Gaithersburg, MD.

Chapter 7

1. Bobbie Reed, *Single Adult Ministry for Today* (St. Louis: Concordia, 1996), 22.
2. This quote and the advantages and disadvantages that follow are taken from ibid.
3. This information and the advantages and disadvantages that follow are taken from ibid., 23.
4. Ibid., 24.
5. Ibid., 141.
6. The advantages and disadvantages that follow are taken from ibid., 24–25.

Chapter 8

1. Bill Flanagan, "Priorities for Singles Ministry," in *Single Adult Ministry*, ed. Jerry Jones (Colorado Springs: Singles Ministry Resources, NavPress, 1991), 45.
2. The four principles are taken from ibid., 44–45.

Chapter 9

1. Doug Fagerstrom, "Questions to Ask before You Start" in Jones's *Growing Your Single Adult Ministry*, 31.

Chapter 10

1. Adapted and modified from Reed, *Single Adult Ministry for Today*, 82.
2. Jones, *Growing Your Single Adult Ministry*, 117.
3. Reed, *Single Adult Ministry for Today*, 89.

Chapter 11

1. Warren Bennis, "What Makes a Leader?" in Jones, *Growing Your Single Adult Ministry*, 83.
2. Bobbie Reed, "How to Retain Single Adults in Leadership Positions," *Enrichment Journal* (Summer 2000), 43.

Resources for Single Adult Ministry

Ministry Websites

Book of Hope—www.bookofhope.com
> The Book of Hope Response Teams equip people to provide God's Word to the youth and children of the world. The group takes teams of young people and adults of all ages all over the world to help distribute the Book of Hope, God's Word, in a dynamic and relevant way to school students. Groups minister using testimonies, drama, music, and multimedia.

Caring Churches—www.caringchurches.com
> A resource for church leaders as they minister to the special needs of those in their churches and communities

Highway Video—www.highwayvideo.com
> Short ministry videos comprised of street interviews and drama skits that drive truth

Love in Action—www.loveinaction.org
> God's intent, his way, for his people—help in overcoming sexual addictions

Mighty River Ministries—www.mightyriver.org

A unique, nondenominational ministry dedicated to serving the body of Christ, Mighty River Ministries has a special branch dedicated to helping young people and single adults of all ages in the area of relationships.

PCs for Pastors—www.PC4P.org

PC4P is a home missions project of the Assemblies of God for single adults that seeks to encourage small churches and new church plants by providing complete computer systems, electronic libraries and study aids, church administration software, and other peripherals.

SAMall—www.singlesmall.com

Resources for the single adult and leader including books and tapes, fund-raising ideas, and associations

Single Life Resources—www.slr.org

Resources from Campus Crusade for Christ for single and single-again adults and their leadership

Strategic Adult Ministry—www.samresources.com

Resources, curriculum, online single adult/young adult magazine, and more from David C. Cook Ministries

Single-Parent Ministry Websites

Beta Family—www.betafamily.com

This site is dedicated to the education and restoration of single-parent families and blended families.

Center for Single Parent Family Ministry—www.spfm.org

This site has ministry activities for children, parents, or families such as single-parent family conferences, retreats for single parents, and seminars for kids.

Cooperative Parenting—www.cooperativeparenting.com

This site has articles and advice for parents as they help their children adjust to divorce.

Dads 4 Life—www.4liferesources.com
This site has articles and many other resources designed to assist the single father to effectively raise his child(ren).

Family Discipleship Ministries—www.parentingministry.org
This site has resources for single parents, their kids, and ministry leaders, including a schedule of seminars for children of single parents.

Hope 4 Single Moms—www.hope4singlemoms.com
This site has articles and many other resources designed to assist the single mother.

Single Parent/Blending Family Tapestry—www.blendingfamily.com
Don and Jenetha Partridge are passionate, experienced authors and speakers who present outstanding information to stepfamilies, blended families, single parents, and single adults dating single parents. Their books and materials are excellent.

Kid's Hope—www.kidshope.org
This site has resources for single parents, their children, and ministry leaders as well as a schedule of seminars for leaders of single-parent family ministries.

Single Parent's Online Retreat—www.singleparent.org
Hosted by a single mother, this site gives book reviews, financial advice, and links to other information.

Blended Family Ministry Websites

Beta Family—www.betafamily.com
This site is dedicated to the education and restoration of single-parent families and blended families.

Crown Financial Ministries—www.crown.org
This site is a ministry providing sound, biblical financial planning and advice.

Growing Kids God's Way—www.gfi.org
This site has curriculum for rearing healthy, godly children and creating balanced families.

Single Parent/Blending Family Tapestry—www.blendingfamily.com
Don and Jenetha Partridge are top-rated speakers who present outstanding information to stepfamilies, blended families, single parents, and single adults dating single parents.

InStep Ministries—www.instepministries.com
Located in Tucson, Arizona, counselor and author Jeff Parziale has created several excellent books and study guides for blended families.

Stepfamily Association of America—www.saafamilies.org
The Stepfamily Association of America is the grandparent organization and resource center for a lot of helpful information. They are also publishers of the bimonthly magazine *Your Stepfamily*.

Single-Again Ministry Websites

Divorce Care—www.divorcecare.com
This site contains a list of support groups and seminars conducted by people who understand the pain of divorce and separation as well as excellent curriculum to help a person heal from the tragedy of divorce.

Divorce Recovery—Christian Divorce Recovery Care Group
www.groups.yahoo.com/group/divorce_recovery
This site is dedicated to fellowship with others who are divorced or directly affected by a divorce.

The Divorce Support Page—www.divorcesupport.com
This is a secular site providing information and resources for the divorcing and newly divorced. Single adult ministry leaders will find information to help members with the legal and emotional fallout from divorce.

Fresh Start Seminars—www.freshstartseminars.org
This is another Christian ministry whose purpose is to touch the lives of the separated and divorced.

GriefShare—www.griefshare.com
This is a site dedicated to finding help as you grieve the loss of a family member or friend.

Marriage Restored—marriagerestored.com
This site offers hope, love, and relationships renewed.

Magazines and Newsletters for Single Adults and Their Leaders

Christian Single—www.lifeway.com/christiansingle
This is a magazine of purposeful living for single adults from the national office of the Southern Baptist Church.
Christian Single
One LifeWay Plaza
Nashville, TN 37234
Beth Clayton, Senior Editor
subscribe@lifeway.com
615-251-5955

Focus on the Family (Single-Parent Family quarterly edition)—www.focusonthefamily.com
This is a magazine from Focus on the Family for single parents. Request the single-parent family edition.
Focus on the Family
8605 Explorer Drive
Colorado Springs, CO 80920-1051

Single Adult Ministries Journal—www.cookministries.com/events/sam_journal
This is a comprehensive online journal for leaders of single adult ministries.
P.O. Box 36670
Colorado Springs, CO 80936
800-487-4726

The Source—www.singles.ag.org—www.youngadults.ag.org
This is a newsletter from the Assemblies of God national office to encourage and equip young adults and single adults and the leaders who work with them.

Single Adult/Young Adult Ministries
1445 N. Boonville Avenue
Springfield, MO 65802
417-862-2781, ext. 4125

Your Stepfamily—www.saafamilies.org
The Stepfamily Association of America is the grandparent organization and resource center for a lot of helpful information. They are also publishers of the bimonthly magazine *Your Stepfamily.*

Leadership/Ministry Books

Barna, George. *Building Effective Lay Leadership Teams.* Ventura, CA: Issachar Resources, 2001.

———. *Single Focus: Understanding Single Adults.* Ventura, CA: Gospel Light, 2003.

———. *Unmarried America: How Singles Are Changing and What It Means for the Church.* Glendale, CA: Barna Research Group, 1993.

Baugh, Ken, and Rich Hurst. *Getting Real.* Colorado Springs: Nav-Press, 2000.

Burns, Bob, and Tom Whitman. *The Fresh Start Divorce Recovery Workbook.* Nashville: Oliver Nelson, 1992.

Church Initiative Inc. *Divorce Care.* Wake Forest, NC, a DVD/video series, 2004.

Cleary, Tim. *The Single Adult Ministry Solution.* Nashville: LifeWay Press, 1996.

Cox, William. *Designing a Single Adult Ministry.* Nashville: Discipleship Resources, 1996.

Cynaumon, Greg. *Helping Single Parents with Troubled Kids.* Colorado Springs: NavPress, 1992.

Fagerstrom, Douglas, ed. *Baker Handbook of Single Adult Ministry.* Grand Rapids: Baker, 1997.

Felts, Stephen. *Start a Revolution: Nine World-Changing Strategies for Single Adults.* Nashville: LifeWay Press, 1996.

Flanagan, Bill. *Counseling Single Adults.* Grand Rapids: Baker, 1996.

———. *Developing a Divorce Recovery Ministry*. Elgin, IL: Singles Ministry Resources, 1994.

Goodall, Wayde. *Enrichment*. Springfield, MO: Gospel Publishing House, 2000.

Harbour, Brian. *Famous Singles of the Bible*. Nashville: Broadman, 1980.

Hsu, Albert Y. *Singles at the Cross-Roads: A Fresh Perspective on Christian Singleness*. Downers Grove, IL: InterVarsity, 1997.

Jones, Jerry. *Growing Your Single Adult Ministry*. Colorado Springs: Cook Communications Ministries, 1993.

———. *The Idea Catalog for Single Adult Ministry*. Colorado Springs: Singles Ministry Resources/NavPress, 1991.

Nilson, Sue, and Andy Morgan. *Starting a Single Adult Ministry*. Colorado Springs: David C. Cook, 1994.

Partridge, Donald. *Single Parents-Savvy Partnering: Stage 1—Dating*. Pleasanton, CA: Ginger Court Press, 2001.

———. *Single Parents-Savvy Partnering: Stage 2—Engagement*. Pleasanton, CA: Ginger Court Press, 2001.

———. *Single Parents-Savvy Partnering: Stage 3—Merging*. Pleasanton, CA: Ginger Court Press, 2001.

Reed, Bobbie. *Baker Handbook of Single Parent Ministry*. Grand Rapids: Baker, 1998.

———. *Single Adult Ministry for Today*. St. Louis: Concordia, 1996.

———. *The Single Parent Journey: 13 Session Study of Needs/Issues/ Solutions*. Anderson, IN: Warner Press, 1992.

Smith, Harold Ivan. *Positively Single*. Minneapolis: Bethany, 1983.

Sprague, Gary. *Kids Hope (Grades 1–5)*. Colorado Springs: Singles Ministry Resources, 1997.

———. *Kids Hope (Grades 6–12)*. Colorado Springs: Singles Ministry Resources, 1997.

Westfall, John, and Bobbie Reed. *Let Go*. San Diego: Single Adult Ministry Resources, 1990.

Wright, Norman. *Before You Remarry: A Guide to Successful Remarriage*. Eugene, OR: Harvest House, 1999.

Leadership Training and Ministry Development for Single Adult Ministry

Assemblies of God—Single Adult/Young Adult Ministries
  Dennis Franck, single adult/young adult ministries director
  Leadership training
  Conferences, seminars, workshops, retreats
  Educating church district offices, church state offices, local churches,
  pastors, and other leaders in Christian ministry
  417-862-2781, ext. 4125
  singles@ag.org
  www.singles.ag.org; www.youngadults.ag.org

Strategic Adult Ministries
  Strategic Adult Ministries provides single adult ministry resources to
  leaders in single adult ministries and young adult ministry resources to
  leaders in young adult ministries. They are also sponsors of the annual
  SAM and Futuregen national leadership conventions, which usually meet
  in March, and they also publish *SAM Journal* (an online magazine).
  Susan Tjaden—events specialist and editor of *SAM Journal*
  www.cookministries.com/events/sam/
  P.O. Box 36670
  Colorado Springs, CO 80936
  800-487-4726

The Singles Network Ministries
Kris Swiatocho
P.O. Box 18598
Asheville, NC 28814
919-779-3686
kris@thesinglesnetwork.org

Denominational Offices for Single Adult/Young Adult Ministries

Assemblies of God
Dennis Franck
Single Adult/Young Adult Ministries Director
1445 N. Boonville Avenue
Springfield, MO 65802
Telephone: 417-862-2781, ext. 4125
singles@ag.org
www.singles.ag.org; www.youngadults.ag.org

Church of God (Cleveland, TN)
Daniel J. Vassell Sr.
Cross Cultural Youth/Single Adult Ministries Coordinator
P.O. Box 2430
Cleveland, TN 37320
Telephone: 423-478-7291
Fax: 423-478-7050
ycecarb@extremegen.org
www.singlesource.cc

Church of the Nazarene
Linda Hardin
Single Adult Ministries Coordinator
6401 The Paseo
Kansas City, MO 64131
Telephone: 816-333-8000, ext. 2257
lhardin@nazarene.org
www.nazarene.org.ssm/s_intro.html

Seventh Day Adventist Church
Barbara Babcock
Coordinator, Adventist Single Adult Ministries (ASAM)
North American Division of the Seventh-day Adventist Church
12501 Old Columbia Pike
Silver Spring, MD 20904-6600
Telephone: 909-954-3153
BBabcockASAM@aol.com
www.adventistsingleadultministries.org

Southern Baptist Church
Morlee Maynard, D.Ed.Min.
Ministry Specialist, Adult Ministry and Church Library
LifeWay Church Resources
One LifeWay Plaza
Nashville, TN 37234-0175
Telephone: 615-251-3640
Fax: 615-251-5618
morlee.maynard@lifeway.com

United Methodist Church
Bill Lizor
Young Adult/Single Adult Ministries Director
P.O. Box 340003
Nashville, TN 37202
Telephone: 877-899-2780, ext. 7005
blizor@gbod.org

United Methodist Church
Julie O'Neal
Faith Formation, Leadership Development and Resource Coordinator with Young Adults
P.O. Box 340003
Nashville, TN 37202
Telephone: 877-899-2780, ext. 7025
joneal@gbod.org

Denominational Offices

Dennis Franck has been leading single adult ministries for more than two decades. He has written many articles and book chapters on the issues of single adult living and ministry and served on the board of the Network of Single Adult Leaders. He is currently the director of Single Adult and Young Adult Ministries for the Assemblies of God.